PRYING OPEN THE DOOR

Foreign Workers in Japan

Takashi Oka

Contemporary Issues Paper #2

CARNEGIE ENDOWMENT FOR INTERNATIONAL PEACE

Copyright© 1994 by the
Carnegie Endowment for International Peace
2400 N Street, N.W., Washington, D.C. 20037

Distributed by the Brookings Institution, Department 029, Washington, D.C., 20042-0029, USA, 1/800-275-1447.

Copy editors: Jeff Porro and Stephanie Terry
Cover: Paddy McLaughlin Concepts & Design

Cover depiction: *From* Horizon (*Winter 1976, volume 8 no.1*), *a silk panel screen of Kyoto, Japan, dated 1614, depicts foreign visitors walking through the capital city.*

Library of Congress Cataloging-in-Publication Data

Oka, Takashi, 1924-
    Prying open the door : foreign workers in Japan / by Takashi Oka.
    p. cm.—(Contemporary issues paper ; #2)
Includes bibliographical references.
ISBN 0-87003-053-1 : $8.95
1. Alien labor—Japan. I. Title. II. Series.
HD8728.5.A2038 1994   94-20944
331.6'2'0952—dc20   CIP

The Carnegie Endowment for International Peace

The Carnegie Endowment for International Peace was established in 1910 in Washington, D.C., with a gift from Andrew Carnegie. As a tax-exempt operating (not grant-making) foundation, the Endowment conducts programs of research, discussion, publication, and education in international affairs and American foreign policy. The Endowment publishes the quarterly magazine *Foreign Policy*.

Carnegie's Senior and Resident Associates, whose backgrounds include government, journalism, law, academia and public affairs, bring to their work substantial firsthand experience in foreign policy through writing, public and media appearances, study groups and conferences. Carnegie associates seek to invigorate and extend both expert and public discussion on a wide range of international issues, including such timely and important subjects as worldwide migration, nonproliferation, regional conflict, multilateralism, democracy-building and the use of force. The Endowment also engages in and encourages projects designed to foster innovative contributions in international affairs.

In 1993 the Endowment opened the Carnegie Russian/Eurasian Center in Moscow. Associates and researchers from Russia and the Newly Independent States are collaborating with Washington associates to enrich intellectual and political discourse on major subjects of common interest.

The Endowment normally does not take institutional positions on public policy issues. It supports its activities principally from its own resources, supplemented by nongovernmental, philanthropic grants.

Table of Contents

Foreword

Japan is at a demographic and labor force crossroads. After recent decades when the number of births was consistently lower than the number of deaths, the Japanese population has been aging at rates matched by few if any other advanced industrial societies. And as the demographic momentum from earlier periods of higher fertility also gradually winds down, Japan is confronting the fact that its citizens are entering the labor force in much smaller numbers. For example, although Japan's labor force grew by nearly 5 million persons between 1984 and 1990, it will grow at about 40 percent of this rate in the 1990s—adding only about 3.1 million workers for the decade.

But even in the labor-tight years of the late 1980s and early 1990s when job openings often exceeded job applicants, Japan was not really facing an "absolute" labor shortage. In fact, unemployment rates among Japan's youngest and oldest workers have been routinely almost twice as high as those for all workers. Furthermore, Japanese women have participated in the labor force at rates that are only about two-thirds those of most advanced industrial societies. Finally, the employment of female workers in service industry jobs (particularly in such areas as direct sales) has remained remarkably "extravagant," at least by Western standards. Clearly, efforts to attract and retain Japan's youngest, oldest, and female workers in the labor market—and more efficiently allocate the labor of women already in the labor force—would expand the supply of labor significantly.

However, neither the government nor the private sector has shown any particular zeal for either rationalizing the overall labor force further or restructuring in any fundamental way that sector of the economy where worker shortages seem to be most pronounced: low value-added businesses and their attendant low-wage labor markets. The measures Japan has contemplated or taken do not go much beyond the by now "traditional" Japanese steps of expanding labor-saving technologies, standardizing parts, and transferring more production and assembly operations abroad.

As a result, the dualism of the Japanese economy continues unabated: at one end there are large, highly automated, high-value-added, high-compensation firms offering lifetime employment; at the other, small and medium-sized firms, often barely visible, offer wages and working conditions increasingly unattractive to many Japanese. Foreign workers, but particularly illegal foreign workers, are especially appealing to those smaller firms precisely because they are willing—even eager—to work with little regard for working conditions and for relatively little money (often half as much as Japanese workers).

Employing illegal foreign workers also allows companies to adjust to demand fluctuations quickly and with few complications. The importance of that feature cannot be overemphasized. Essentially bereft of rights, foreign workers are expendable in a culture that still prescribes lifelong employer/employee relationships for its citizens. They provide marginal firms with an essential lifeline.

At the same time, however, the presence of illegal foreign workers not only creates the conditions for the social and cultural backlash so vividly described by Mr. Oka, but also, in a perverse way, helps postpone Japan's adoption of the restructuring measures that are at the heart of open and competitive economies. Two of the most obvious such measures are making much greater and more rational use of female labor and bringing into the labor force such grossly underutilized groups as older Japanese and the handicapped.

Two reasons seem to be at the core of the Japanese reluctance to explore more systematically the labor market potential of these groups. The first is cultural and applies particularly to women. The aggressive employment of women would be a radical departure from what is presently culturally acceptable in Japan. The second is much more practical. Japanese employers are clearly not eager to invest in the retraining and employment of older and handicapped workers, or, for that matter, young women. Such investments are thought to have decidedly small (or, in the case of women, uncertain) economic returns.

However, even though the recession has noticeably eased Japan's worker crunch, the demographic day of reckoning cannot be avoided. By early in the next century, if not before, Japan's labor shortages will force it either to pursue a culturally painful labor force rationalization, or simply to turn entire labor market segments over to foreign workers. (Reversing the demographic trend is not a serious prospect, nor could it make a difference for at least a generation.) In either case, and as Mr. Oka makes clear, Japan must *now* begin to address the issue of its intolerance toward both non-Japanese and returning ethnic Japanese.

Among the former, Japan's Korean minority is especially important because it leads a segregated and marginal existence despite its presence in Japan for several generations, as Mr. Oka documents so sensitively and convincingly. Among the latter, most notable are the returning ethnic Japanese who come primarily from Brazil but also from such other Latin American countries as Peru and Argentina, as well as from Asian countries occupied by Japan in the 1930s and 1940s. These ethnic Japanese have been flooding back to Japan during the last few years only to face social and cultural ostracism, inferior social and economic rights, and no clear-cut citizenship rules.

The economy is imposing its cold rationality about the need for workers on an insular culture so protective of its distinctness (as shown by the remarkable increase in illegal foreign workers so definitively documented in Mr. Oka's essay). As it does so, one might have expected the Japanese government to be offering the public a crash course in how to prepare socioculturally and politically for the acceptance of low-skilled and unskilled foreign workers. Yet, one does not discern an effort to match the gravity of the challenge.

This is not to say that no effort has been made. However, the one outlined below has faltered as the recession has attenuated the worker crunch. And as might be expected, both the process of deciding on a low-skill–level "guestworker" program and that of generating "consensus" about it are quintessentially Japanese.

First, the Japanese government studied immigration systems of several Western countries closely. Two systems were of particular interest to the Japanese: the U.S. system's "nonimmigrant" (i.e., temporary immigration) components and Germany's guestworker policies.

Second, an immigration law was enacted in 1990 facilitating the temporary, if often long-term, immigration of highly skilled workers—an issue of economic priority for any nation. The act was modelled almost exclusively on U.S. law, but prohibited the importation of low and unskilled foreign workers.

Third, an intense, yet discreet, debate commenced within the relevant government ministries—Foreign Affairs, MITI, Labor, and Justice—focusing particularly on the economic implications of Japan's demographic deficit and the ensuing labor shortages. Energizing that debate were official projections pointing to worker deficits as high as 4 million by the end of the century, almost half of them in such key sectors as the computer industry. Assuming even the most aggressive automation and "out-sourcing," those numbers could be reduced only by half.

Fourth, government analyses reached a preliminary conclusion that some kind of program for importing unskilled workers was probably unavoidable. That conclusion was validated by an extraordinary fact: despite a Draconian ban against employing low- and unskilled foreign workers, even official estimates pointed to a near-tripling of the illegal foreign worker population since 1990.

Finally, a tentative decision was reached to explore politically how to organize the importation of low- and unskilled foreign workers. The first steps in that effort were to float the decision to import workers as a trial-balloon both domestically and internationally; design the appropriate recruitment and importation scheme (built around the concept of "training"); and devise ways to legitimize any ensuing program both at home and abroad.

The domestic effort focused on seeking consensus for the decision by managing perceptions and orchestrating public events, usually through the use of "proxy" non-governmental organizations and interest groups that advocated, respectively, foreign worker rights and a guestworker policy.

The international effort included replacing dormancy—even unin-
terest—with intense activism in international discussions about
immigration and seeking (even cultivating) the endorsement of leading foreign immigration experts for the course of action Japan contemplated. In both instances, the effort showcased the Japanese proposals' emphasis on the "training" of foreign workers. That focus
presented the program as a significant contribution to the developed
world's efforts to use "training through migration" as a key development tool for countries that export workers.

The slackening in the demand for labor because of the recession
has led to a sharp pause in Japan's efforts to prepare for increased
immigration. It has also clearly given those opposed to relaxing the
prohibition against the importation of low- and unskilled workers
(led by the Justice and Labor Ministries) an opportunity to raise anew
and with additional vigor their sociocultural and, as Mr. Oka makes
clear, budgetary concerns about such a policy.

This pause, however, should not be mistaken as evidence that
culture either has already or will necessarily prevail over economic
need. In fact, there should be little doubt that economic rationality
will prevail over the more extreme expressions of cultural intolerance.
Japan *will* become more ethnically and racially diverse—although
there will be resistance to becoming more tolerant or plural in spirit.

Mr. Oka's essay sheds much-needed light on Japanese thinking
and practices toward foreign workers (and minorities more generally)—issues about which most Western specialists know very little.
In fact, Japan is still held up by many observers as an example of an
economy that has managed well without relying on foreign workers.
Mr. Oka's careful account of the Japanese debate about immigration
and his insights about the human rights challenges that immigration
forces upon Japan become the proper backdrop for his principal
recommendation: Japan should develop an "overall plan on migration" in cooperation with other industrial democracies. Following
this suggestion might in fact serve us all well.

Yet perhaps the essay's greatest value lies in the pointed questions
it raises about Japan's lack of preparations to open itself up socially
and culturally. The question of how Japan might adapt once again

and allow economic rationality to determine its policies toward immigration—and whether it will succeed in its efforts—is one of the most interesting policy and political issues in the migration field in the years ahead.

In Western models, as societies become more diverse, economic, political, and social power also diversify and become more inclusive (recent events in Europe notwithstanding). The Japanese variant, however, is likely to seek to maintain power in the hands of Japanese as long as possible. In doing so, the Japanese would in some ways become the modern-day version of classical Sparta and Athens. As with ancient Sparta, Japan would assign many of the society's low-level tasks (what the Japanese call—translated into English— the "three Ds": "dangerous," "dirty," and "difficult") to a class of modern-day helots from the region. And much like ancient Athens, Japan would simultaneously create a class of high-level foreign workers to engage in a variety of specialized tasks. In this scenario, Japan might continue to remain an economic powerhouse and yet appear to be virtually impervious to demographic destiny. Of course, in the long run, none of us really are.

Demetrios G. Papademetriou
Senior Associate & Director

Immigration Policy Program
Carnegie Endowment for International Peace
September 1994

CHAPTER 1

Introduction

Japan is an island of affluence in a sea of Asian poverty, but its 124 million people face a growing dilemma: how can they reconcile their desire to maintain a cozy, consensual island society with their need for foreign workers willing to perform tasks that most Japanese avoid? Such jobs are what the Japanese call "3-K" (or, in English, "3-D") jobs—dirty (*kitanai*), difficult (*kitsui*), and dangerous (*kiken*).

This report focuses on Japanese policies toward foreign workers. It describes traditional Japanese attitudes toward foreigners, the changes brought about by economic prosperity and by demographics, the main ethnic groups in the growing foreign labor force, and the public reactions and debate caused by the increasing foreign presence. It concludes with policy recommendations.

The Japanese still see themselves as a homogeneous people, speaking the same language and sharing patterns of social behavior developed over centuries of relative isolation on a group of islands 100 miles off the coast of Asia. To preserve that homogeneity, official immigration policies make it all but impossible for unskilled workers to enter Japan, except for ethnic Japanese or their families. But the desire for homogeneity conflicts with growing economic needs as the population ages, work habits change, and labor shortages develop in the 3-D jobs.

Japan is the seventh most populous country in the world, but its demographics are changing rapidly. With life expectancy at seventy-nine years, the Japanese are living longer and producing fewer babies (1.5 babies per couple in 1992). If present trends continue, Japan's population will start declining about the year 2010. In addition, if the tendency of Japanese workers to avoid 3-D jobs continues or accelerates, the foreign component of Japan's population is bound to increase.

In fact, using various loopholes in the law, a stream of economic migrants has been entering Japan since the mid-1980s, sparking a growing debate among scholars, opinion leaders, and the media. A spate of books and articles describes controversies over foreign workers in Western Europe and the United States and suggests what lessons Japan should draw from them. While no one advocates unrestricted immigration, opinion ranges from demands for draconian enforcement of existing laws, including the expulsion of illegal workers, to calls for the legalization of those illegal immigrants already in Japan.

As of December 31, 1992, the number of foreigners legally residing in Japan totaled 1,281,644—45 percent more than in 1987, according to Justice Ministry figures. The overwhelming majority— 1,000,673—were from Asia.

Most registered foreigners are either permanent residents or residents intending to stay longer than the ninety days usually granted to bona fide tourists. Most illegal foreigners (not included in official figures above), entered Japan on ninety-day tourist visas or on fifteen-day shore passes, then found jobs, usually in the 3-D category, and overstayed. Professor Hiroshi Komai of Tsukuba University refers to them as "rule-violaters, not criminals"—a distinction that the police also make implicitly, though not explicitly.

Because unskilled foreign workers arrived in Japan more recently than in Europe or the United States, their numbers are more modest. Among a total 1991 population of 124,452,000 and a work force of 50,020,000, Japan has a foreign work force that, according to Justice Ministry figures, totals roughly 600,000. Of these, ethnic Japanese number nearly 150,000, skilled workers slightly more than 150,000, and illegal workers—almost all unskilled—nearly 300,000. More specifically, the most recent (November 1, 1993) Justice Ministry figures show there were 296,751 illegal workers in Japan, or 0.6 percent fewer than there had been six months earlier—the first time there

Figure 1. Illegal Immigrants in Japan

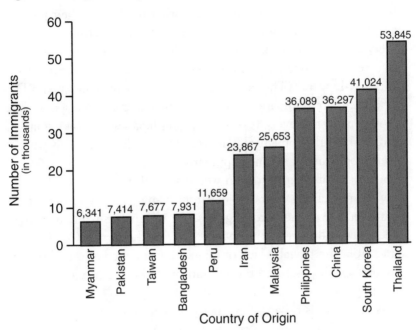

(As of November 1993 according to Ministry of Justice figures.)

had been a decline, however slight, in those figures. Figure 1 provides statistics on illegal immigrants in Japan by country of origin.

To those figures should be added nearly 50,000 students who work practically full-time, although they must attend four hours of language classes per day to keep their visas.

It should be noted that those figures may not tell the whole story. The Immigration Bureau of the Ministry of Justice keeps semiannual statistics on the number of illegal workers and their countries of origin. But the statistics register only the number of such foreigners who turn themselves in to the Immigration Bureau, and some scholars point out that the actual number must be much higher.

The official number of illegal workers has risen dramatically since the late 1980s, from 32,000 in 1986 to 106,000 in 1990 to 298,646 in May 1993—an almost tenfold increase in seven years. The decline to 296,751 in November 1993 reflects the severity of Japan's current recession. It also shows, however, that while some foreign workers are out of work, most have managed either to cling to their jobs or to find lower-paying new ones. There has also been no public outcry that foreign workers are taking jobs from the Japanese, which indicates that foreigners are not competing with Japanese workers for non-3-D work. (The Japanese have not totally abandoned 3-D work; there are occupations such as municipal garbage disposal that are well-paid. But every year fewer young Japanese are taking up such work. If the foreigners compete with the Japanese, it is with older people and part-timers, primarily women.)

Since the number of foreign workers is still relatively small and they are not taking desirable jobs from many Japanese citizens, the controversy over their growing presence in Japan is really over the effect they will have on Japanese society in the future. Complaints range from the trivial—lack of etiquette in public baths and unsanitary garbage disposal—to the substantive—the rise in violent crime and drug use.

As yet there is no anti-foreigner political movement in Japan like the ones that have swept across parts of Europe, although the rightist fringe has taken to shouting anti-foreign slogans. For now, the argument is between those who would hold the "barbarians" outside the gate at all costs (*sakoku*) and those who believe Japan must open its doors, at least to a limited degree, by relaxing draconian laws barring foreign unskilled workers (*kaikoku*). *Sakoku*, meaning closed country, and *kaikoku*, meaning open country, are terms taken from the debate that raged among Japanese officials and intellectuals in the mid-nineteenth century over whether Japan should remain in feudal isolation or open its borders and try to catch up with the West.

Like Europe, Japan sent out migrants in the late nineteenth and early twentieth centuries, rather than receiving them. Emigrants went out from Japan again, mainly toward Latin America, in the early postwar years. Only in the last decade or so have foreign workers begun arriving in Japan in noticeable numbers.

The Japanese who complain about that, however, have a selective view of their own history, forgetting that during the period they occupied Korea and Taiwan as colonies, people from those territories came to Japan as hewers of wood and drawers of water. They also fail to realize that their hostility toward the current wave of Asian workers flowing into Japan has been conditioned by the way they perceived and treated earlier immigrants.

CHAPTER 2

The Historical Framework: Modernization and Change

The popular Japanese view of themselves as an ethnically homogeneous people is not historically accurate. Like most other nations, the Japanese are a mixture of several ethnic groupings. The major differences are between the tall, light-skinned, horse-riding people who reached the islands from Korea and the shorter, browner tribes who migrated northwards from South China and Southeast Asia. Homogeneity did develop early, however, because of Japan's relatively isolated geographic position as a string of islands off the Asian mainland.

Nevertheless, until the two centuries of isolation imposed by the feudal Tokugawa Shoguns—from 1636 until U.S. Commodore Matthew Perry's forcible opening of Japan in 1854—there were regular, though limited, contacts between Japan and the mainland. In the fourteenth and fifteenth centuries, Japanese pirates known as *wako* ravaged the coasts of China. In the sixteenth and early seventeenth centuries, there were Japanese communities in Macao and Southeast Asia. Similarly, there were Chinese and Koreans who settled in Japan during that time, some voluntarily, some as the result of conquest.

After that relatively open period, however, the isolation of the Tokugawa period was nearly total and has had a lasting effect on the psyche of the Japanese people. For two centuries, anyone caught leaving or returning to Japan was executed. There was room for discretion only in the case of sailors blown off course. The Tokugawas imposed a rigid feudal hierarchy on the country, but their rule was also a time of peace, relative prosperity, and cultural flowering.

Perry's ships arrived as the Shogunate was beginning to crumble because of internal conflicts. His message that Japan had to open its doors caused an intense debate between those who wanted to continue in feudal isolation (*sakoku*) and those who wanted to open the country (*kaikoku*). The *kaikoku* advocates won, leading to the downfall of the Tokugawas. In the Meiji Restoration of 1868, a group of young, modernizing samurai took power in the name of the emperor. The use of the nineteenth-century terms *sakoku* and *kaikoku* is an indication that the Japanese do not view the current immigration controversy in isolation, but as an integral part of the larger historical argument over how open a country Japan should be.

The Meiji oligarchs closed the door on Japan's feudal period and ushered in a new era of frenzied catching up with the West. During the Meiji period (1868–1912), Japan became a modern nation on the Western model. But many of the attitudes of self-containment and rigid hierarchy developed during the preceding two centuries remained, even amid the new openness to fresh breezes from the West.

As they Westernized and modernized, the Meiji oligarchs fostered the perception that the Japanese were a homogeneous people, different from their Asian neighbors and from Americans or Europeans. According to Komai,[1] they sought in part to justify the new government's absorption of the Ainus in Hokkaido in 1869 and of the Ryukyu kingdom (also known as Okinawa) in 1879.

The transition from feudalism to a more open, competitive political and economic system and the accompanying monetarization of the rural economy brought hard times to Japan's peasantry. In the latter half of the nineteenth century, the country became an exporter of its citizenry to the sugar plantations of Hawaii, to the U.S. mainland, and to Latin America. Emigration to Latin America, especially to Brazil, accelerated after 1924, the year the U.S. Congress passed legislation setting immigration quotas based on national origins. The new laws excluded Asians, who were already ineligible for citizenship on racial grounds. The Japanese also emigrated to Micronesia, which came under Japanese control after World War I.

A different kind of emigration took place to Taiwan, annexed from China in 1895, and to Korea, occupied in the early 1900s and annexed in 1910. The Japanese went to those two territories as officials, businessmen, hangers-on, and carpetbaggers.

After Japan embarked on its military adventures in Manchuria in the early 1930s, hundreds of thousands of Japanese farmers were also resettled in the bleak plains of Northern Manchuria. Many were killed during the Soviet invasion at the end of World War II. Survivors returned to Japan bitter and disillusioned.

While Japanese were leaving their homeland, Koreans and Chinese—mostly Taiwanese—were immigrating to Japan. The inflow increased dramatically during World War II, when Japan suffered labor shortages because so many able-bodied young men were in the armed forces. Koreans, and to a lesser extent mainland Chinese, were rounded up and forced to work in factories, coal mines, and on construction projects, often under appalling conditions.

After Japan's defeat, most of the Chinese and many of the Koreans were repatriated, but large numbers remained. Japanese postwar attitudes toward foreigners, especially toward Asian workers, were conditioned largely by the presence of the Korean minority—about 830,000 individuals, including naturalized Japanese citizens—and by the political and social controversies that presence caused.

As Japan's economy recovered in the 1950s and 1960s and reached unprecedented heights of prosperity in the 1970s, emigration, which had never been on the scale of that of a Greece or an Ireland, dwindled. Population growth slowed, and labor shortages began to occur, first in small workshops and in the service industries, then in construction, and eventually in the larger industrial establishments.

In Europe, under similar circumstances, industries imported foreign workers. West Germany recruited workers from Yugoslavia and Turkey. France and Great Britain imported workers from former Asian or African colonies. Japanese businessmen and government officials vowed they would never follow suit. They claimed that Japan's economic prowess derived in large part from the homogeneity of its people, and they encouraged companies to automate and to use robots rather than to depend on cheap imported labor.

Yet within the economy, some important industries continued to find it difficult to attract job seekers while others were unsuitable for automation: service industries such as restaurants and laundries; construction and civil engineering, an industry consisting of a few large companies that subcontracted work to innumerable small ones; and manufacturers with 3-D jobs, such as foundries, painting, and various types of metalworking.

Although such firms were often just workshops, they were the bottom rungs of a long ladder of subcontractors that reached up to some of the top names in Japanese industry—Nissan, Toyota, and Sanyo, for example. As the employees of those subcontractors aged in the 1980s, a trickle of male workers from the Philippines, Thailand, and other Asian countries began to filter in.

In 1985, Japan's Finance Minister, at a meeting in New York with his colleagues from Britain, France, Germany, and the U.S. (the so-called Plaza Agreement), agreed to let the U.S. dollar float lower against the yen in order to help the flagging U.S. economy. In two years the yen was worth twice what it had been in dollar terms, which meant Japanese salaries were also worth twice as much. As a result, the influx of foreign workers rose. The rate of immigration still remained far below that in Europe. But it was alarming to the Japanese, who did not have much contact with foreigners except as tourists, businesspeople, or students.

Japan had reciprocal agreements with many Asian countries, including Pakistan, Bangladesh, and Iran, allowing bona fide tourists to visit without a visa. Asian economic migrants took advantage of those agreements to enter Japan in the guise of tourists, who were eligible to stay for up to three months. Once they passed safely through entrance procedures at Narita Airport, they disappeared into the underground economy.

For the first time in its history, Japan had a problem with foreign workers who came to Japan to stay.

CHAPTER 3

Koreans in Japan: The Oldest Foreign Community

Koreans form the oldest and largest foreign community in Japan. At the end of 1992, according to Ministry of Justice figures, 688,144 Koreans had registered with town and city officials as foreign residents. About two-thirds of those hold South Korean passports, while one-third hold North Korean passports or are loyal to North Korea. In addition, there are approximately 150,000 Japanese citizens of Korean ancestry—people who have either become naturalized or who are the descendants of naturalized Japanese. Overall, it is estimated that the ethnic Korean community in Japan, including Koreans who may never have bothered to register with the authorities, totals somewhat less than 1 million people, or about 0.8 percent of the total Japanese population.

Japan annexed Korea in 1910 and ruled it as a colony until August 15, 1945, when Emperor Hirohito announced Japan's surrender to the Allies in World War II. The Japanese policy can be summed up as one of assimilation, a policy similar to that pursued by the French in Algeria, but carried out much more thoroughly. Whereas the French seemed satisfied with ensuring that those individuals under its tutelage accepted French culture, official Japanese doctrine held that Japanese and Koreans were one race.

Koreans were to be referred to as "peninsulars," not by their ethnic name. Universal education was introduced, but the language of instruction was Japanese; Koreans caught speaking Korean to each other in school were punished. (The same policy was applied to Okinawans, who speak an old dialect of Japanese.)

"State Shinto" was introduced to Korea as the official Japanese dogma. State Shinto holds that all Japanese are in effect one family, descended from the Sun Goddess or her relatives and retainers, and that the emperor is the head of the family. Japan insisted that State Shinto was not a religion and that Christians should bow at Shinto shrines as a sign of respect, not of worship. Many Korean Christians were questioned by police or arrested for refusing to comply.

But the most hated aspect of the Japanese assimilation policy was a decree published during World War II that forced Koreans to take Japanese surnames. Earlier, the practice had been encouraged but was voluntary. Many Koreans committed suicide rather than give up their family names.

Because life in Korea was hard, a number of Koreans took advantage of the Japanese citizenship imposed on them and moved to Japan where they generally landed at the bottom of society. They tended to work as launderers, junk men, charcoal makers, garbage collectors, miners, and on construction crews. Ordinary Japanese looked down on them as poor, uneducated, and dirty. In times of crisis, as in the aftermath of Tokyo's Great Earthquake of 1923, they became the victims of Japanese mobs. But Koreans residing in Japan could participate in local and national elections, and one Korean living in Tokyo managed to be elected a member of the Imperial Diet.

In 1909, a year before Japan annexed Korea, 790 Koreans lived in Japan. Two years later, there were 2,527. By 1919, a year that saw the first mass demonstrations in Korea for independence, there were 30,189 Koreans in Japan. By 1930, the number had grown to 298,091. By 1940, when Japan began to face labor shortages because of wartime mobilization, there were 1,190,444. During World War II, more Koreans were brought to Japan as forced laborers. In 1944, the Korean population in Japan peaked at 1,936,843.[2]

After Japan's surrender, Korea was freed from Japanese rule but became a victim of the Cold War. Korea was divided at the 38th parallel with Soviet troops in the north and the Americans in the south. Koreans in Japan ceased to be Japanese subjects, and large numbers of them were repatriated to their homeland. Those that remained were classified at first as "third-country nationals" because they were neither Japanese nor citizens of the victorious Allies. The contest between communist North Korea and noncommunist South Korea, both officially created in 1948, was carried into Japan. Competing organizations were set up—Chosoren (The General Association of Korean Residents in Japan), loyal to North Korea, and Mindan, owing allegiance to South Korea.

Although the overwhelming majority of Koreans in Japan were from the southern part of the Korean peninsula, North Korean agents penetrated the Korean community in Japan earlier and much more effectively than the South Korean government apparatus. They set up schools and youth organizations and created the image of a North Korean motherland eager to welcome her sons and daughters. In the first years after World War II, approximately 100,000 Koreans in Japan were voluntarily repatriated to North Korea on ships sent by the Pyongyang government. More recently, the number of Koreans choosing to "go home" to North Korea has dwindled to ten or fewer per year.

Before the death of Kim Il Sung, Chosoren ran a kindergarten-through-university school system in the islands teaching loyalty to the dictator and his son, Kim Jong Il, to the one-third of the Korean population in Japan who retained their loyalty to the North. Mindan by contrast has only four primary schools in the country—two in Osaka and one each in Tokyo and Kyoto.

The San Francisco peace treaty ending the Allied occupation of Japan was signed in September 1951 when the Korean War was at its height. Moscow refused to attend the peace conference, and neither North Korea nor South Korea were invited. Japan did not regularize relations with South Korea until 1965; it still has no official relations with North Korea, although emissaries of the two governments meet by agreement in Beijing.

The 1965 treaty with Seoul gave Korean residents in Japan and their children the status of permanent resident, with the option of becoming Japanese citizens. The two sides agreed to confer again in 1991 on the status of the residents' grandchildren. Because Japan follows the rule of *jus sanguinis*, citizenship by the nationality of the parents, rather than that of *jus solis*, citizenship by place of birth, being born in Japan does not automatically confer citizenship, even on Koreans who may have lived in the country for three or four generations and who may speak no other language than Japanese. Naturalization is an arduous process, and until 1985, everyone undergoing this process, Korean or otherwise, had to adopt a Japanese surname expressible in *kanji*, Chinese characters.

At the time of the 1965 treaty, both Tokyo and Seoul expected that by 1991 most Koreans residing in Japan would either have become Japanese citizens or would have returned to Korea. As a result, the question of what to do about their grandchildren would probably be academic. In fact, however, far more Koreans have retained their nationality and remained permanent residents than have become Japanese citizens. Among these permanent residents, the question of surnames has become a much discussed issue.

As noted earlier, during the period of Japanese rule, Koreans were forced to adopt Japanese surnames. After Korea's liberation, most Koreans living in Japan reverted to their original surnames, but many continued to use their Japanese surnames as well. Since Koreans and Japanese have no real physical differences, it was easy for a Korean using a Japanese surname to pass as Japanese. For some, whose careers in business or in entertainment depended on being accepted as Japanese, the practice was a necessity.

In 1970 the Park Chong Sok case became a cause célèbre. Park, a 19-year-old Korean born and brought up in Japan, used his Japanese name, Shoji Arai, to apply for a job at a software plant in Yokohama owned by the electronics and machinery conglomerate Hitachi. He passed a stiff entrance examination and was accepted as an employee, only to be rejected when it was discovered that he was a Korean citizen whose legal name was Park. The young man charged discrimination, demanded to be employed under his legal name, and took his case to court in December that year. He was supported by a number of Japanese, including college students and his landlady, who formed an "Aid Mr. Park Group."

On June 19, 1974, the Yokohama District Court upheld the young man's right both to be employed and to use his legal, Korean name. Hitachi decided not to appeal and formally accepted Park as an employee. In 1990 Park, who has been a Hitachi employee since the 1974 decision, gave a party to celebrate his years with the company and to thank all the people who had supported him.

Had the company not required identity papers giving Park's legal, Korean surname, he might have spent his whole career at Hitachi under his Japanese name. As one of Park's supporters wrote, "The Hitachi case not only questioned Japanese society but was a means for Park himself to regain his own identity."[3] Park's action gave other Koreans courage to to follow his example. However, Mindan estimates that 90 percent of Korean residents of Japan still use their Japanese surnames.

Until 1985, the Koreans who had become Japanese citizens were, like other foreign residents, forced to adopt Japanese surnames as part of the naturalization process. The 1985 revision of the nationality law gave all naturalized citizens the option of retaining their foreign names. The overwhelming majority still adopt Japanese names as a practical necessity for getting along in Japanese society.

In the 1980s the issue of fingerprinting became a prime example of Japanese discrimination against foreigners in general and Koreans in particular. The government requires all foreign residents over the age of sixteen to be fingerprinted. The general complaint by foreigners against the fingerprinting requirement, which was introduced while Japan was under American occupation after World War II, is that it treats foreigners as potential criminals: the only Japanese who are fingerprinted are those who have gotten in trouble with the police. The Korean community is particularly sensitive on this point because it is by far the largest group of non-Japanese residing in Japan.

Furthermore, many Korean residents were born and have grown up in Japan. They have Japanese surnames, attend Japanese schools, and in some cases may not even know that they are legally Korean, not Japanese. Those young people often found the process traumatic. They suddenly had to go to city hall at the age of sixteen to be fingerprinted, and then they were issued an alien registration card to be carried with them at all times. (Police have a right to demand the card and to impose a penalty on those who do not have it on them.) In addition, the fingerprinting had to be repeated every time the alien registration card was renewed, at first every three years, then every five years.

The first Korean resident to refuse to be fingerprinted was Han Jeong Sok in September 1980. Born in 1928, brought to Japan by his parents at the age of nine, Han said he had been fingerprinted many times without protest, but that one day he thought he would at least like to spare his children and grandchildren the humiliation. Han had visions of being deported or of being taken to court, but to his surprise the ward office to which he went gave him a new registration card despite his refusal to be fingerprinted.[4]

Other Koreans began to do the same, and some of them were taken to court. Japanese sympathizers took up their cases as a human rights issue, and young Koreans themselves demonstrated widely throughout Japan for the fingerprinting requirement to be abolished. In Korea the issue generated massive publicity as an illustration of continuing Japanese arrogance and discrimination.

By the mid-1980s, South Korea was no longer an impoverished Asian backwater but a vibrant, growing presence in the world economy and, for Japan, a neighbor whose goodwill was important. Although the police and the Ministry of Justice in Japan argued strongly for keeping the fingerprinting requirement, it was diluted in 1987. It was made a one-time-only requirement for all foreigners, and in 1992 it was abolished entirely for Koreans who were permanent residents of Japan. However, Japan continues to require all foreigners, except those on tourist or government visas, to register as aliens and to carry their alien registration cards with them.

Finally, in addition to permanent residents, there are more than 40,000 Koreans in Japan who are illegal aliens. They entered Japan after World War II, many of them in recent years. Their motives are similar to those of other illegal aliens—to earn as much money as possible as quickly as possible. Most are in typical 3-D work such as construction.

CHAPTER 4

The Chinese: Future Threat?

The Chinese are the second largest and fastest growing foreign community in Japan. The number of Koreans legally residing in Japan has grown slowly over the years and has changed very little in recent years. The number of Chinese, on the other hand, has quadrupled during the past quarter century (see Table 1).

The Japanese view of the Chinese community is rooted in history and geography and complicated by the turbulent unfolding of political and economic ties in recent decades. Historically, the Japanese have viewed the Chinese much as they have viewed the Koreans, but with more respect. China is not only far bigger and more powerful than Korea, it has also been the source of major strands of philosophy and religion that have taken root in Japan. China has been an important influence in the arts, from painting, sculpture, and ceramics to landscape gardening and the tea ceremony. As in the case of

Table 1. Korean and Chinese Residents in Japan

	LEGAL RESIDENTS			
	1969	1990	1992	
Koreans	603,712	687,940	688,144	
Chinese	51,448	150,339	195,334	

	ILLEGAL RESIDENTS			
				(1993)
Koreans	n.a.	35,687	35,687	41,024
Chinese	n.a	10,039	25,737	36,297

(Source: Ministry of Justice, Japan)

Koreans, there was an exchange of visitors between Japan and China throughout the centuries, with Chinese priests, scholars, and merchants settling in Japan from time to time.

Once Japan entered the modern world in the mid-nineteenth century, however, it progressed more rapidly than China. In 1894–95 Japan defeated China in a brief war. Japan soon adopted the same colonialist and imperialist attitudes toward China that it accused the Western powers of harboring toward Japan. The Japanese took over Taiwan in 1895 and the southern tip of the Liaodong Peninsula ten years later. They invaded Manchuria in 1931 and then the rest of China beginning in 1937.

Defeat in World War II, with China one of the victorious allies, and the subsequent emergence of the communist People's Republic of China have caused mixed feelings among the Japanese. To some extent, the nostalgia for China and its classical traditions—viewed by most Japanese much as Britons view ancient Greece and Rome—survives, coupled with a sense of guilt over Japanese aggression against China. Stronger, however, is the feeling that although the Chinese people remain poor and backward, their sheer numbers—ten times Japan's population—and the increasing military strength of the People's Republic make them a potential threat: they must be handled with care. This feeling is reflected in Japanese attitudes toward the Chinese in their midst—a mingling of condescension and respect.

As Japan emerged from feudal isolation in the mid-nineteenth century, the Chinese began to come to Japan on a more regular basis. The Chinese settled in the treaty ports of Kobe and Yokohama as merchants, seamen, clerks in British companies, and servants to Western residents. They established modest Chinatowns and intermarried extensively with the Japanese. Sadaharu Oh, the popular Japanese baseball star, is from one such immigrant family, the Chinese reading of his name being Wang Zhenzhi.

After China ceded Taiwan to Japan in 1895, the Taiwanese became Japanese citizens and, like the Koreans, some settled in Japan. They did not restrict themselves to the Chinatowns as had the mainland

Table 2. Major Categories of Chinese Legally Resident in Japan

(As of December 1992)

1. Permanent residents *(mostly descended from Chinatown residents and other long-time settlers)*	20,714
2. Spouses and dependents *(mostly dependents of Japanese repatriates)*	29,008
3. Long-term residents *(Chinese relatives of Japanese repatriates)*	23,877

Categories 2 and 3 are expected to increase because as each newly arrived relative qualifies to become a long-term or permanent resident, he may in turn bring his relatives into Japan.

4. Students *(University and college level)*	31,910
5. Students *(Language and other special schools)*	33,962
6. Trainees	10,185

Categories 4, 5, and 6 are expected to produce the bulk of overstayers.

Chinese. Like the Koreans, the Taiwanese lost their Japanese citizenship after Japan's defeat in World War II and the restitution of Taiwan to China.

Neither the Taiwanese nor the Chinatown Chinese communities in Japan have grown much in recent years. The recent increase in the Chinese presence in Japan is due to two new groups: Chinese dependents of Japanese repatriates from China (mostly Manchuria), who came under a program that began in 1975; and overstayers. The latter are Chinese who, like other Asians, came to Japan as students or trainees and remained in the country after their authorized period of residence expired (see Table 2).

Since the Chinese, like the Koreans, look similar to the Japanese and learn the language with relative ease, they have not been as conspicuous to the public as have the Pakistanis, the Bangladeshis, and the Iranians whose arrival in the mid-1980s made many Japanese conscious, for the first time, that large numbers of foreign workers were living in Japan. The facility with which the Chinese learn the Japanese language also makes them more likely than other Asians to enter Japan as students or as trainees. Almost 57 percent of college-level foreign students and 73 percent of language school and other special school students come from China. In addition, many students from Thailand or Malaysia are of Chinese ethnic origin.

Students in Japanese colleges must take a regular course of studies. As mentioned earlier in this text, students in language schools, many of whom have come to work rather than to study, must spend at least four hours per day, five days a week, in language school. For many years, language schools were one legal way that people seeking work could enter Japan. As a consequence, the government has become very strict in supervising them.

Box 1. Foreign "Students" in Japan.

One student I know attends language school from 9 a.m. to 1 p.m., Monday through Friday. From 2 p.m. to 10 p.m. every day, seven days a week, the student is a waiter in a hotel, earning 200,000 yen* ($1,800) per month. He has a bona fide guarantor, a Japanese citizen who, according to law, must have a declared income of at least 8 million yen ($72,000) per year. Every student must have such a guarantor. According to police sources, however, a well-organized network of Chinese and Japanese brokers can supply all the required documentation and travel expenses for fees of several million yen, fees that will be repaid from the student's earnings.

This student knows others who have no intention of going to college and instead will become illegal residents when they have completed the two-year language school course.

*Throughout the text, yen-dollar conversions are based on a rate of 110 yen = $1. This rate prevailed during much of the period of this research.

Analysts of immigration trends point out that the Chinese could become by far the largest foreign community in Japan. There is a widespread fear, particularly among government officials, that if China goes through a new cataclysm similar to the Cultural Revolution of 1966–76, the result would be a tsunami of refugees that would overwhelm Japan's resources. The $800 million of economic aid that

Tokyo provides annually to China is designed in part to avoid such a disaster by keeping China growing economically and stable politically. Nevertheless, the Japanese recognize that emigration pressures in China are bound to increase because of demographics and Beijing's inability to keep up with popular expectations.

One long-time police expert on China, who wishes to remain anonymous because of his continued ties with the intelligence community, says that Beijing's economic reform policies have made it much easier for Chinese who want to leave the country to do so. The drab lives most Chinese still lead, coupled with pervasive television images of life in Western countries and in Japan, have become a powerful incentive for young Chinese to emigrate, particularly those in coastal provinces like Fujian and Guangdong. For most, the ideal destination is America; but Japan is closer and not quite so foreign.

If Chinese citizens cannot leave China legally as students or perhaps as spouses—Chinese brokers in Shanghai and other major cities can arrange brides for Japanese males—they might try smuggling themselves aboard fishing vessels and other small craft chartered by brokers.

The smuggling business, according to the police expert, is a three-country affair: mainland China (the ports of exit being in Guangdong or Fujian provinces), Taiwan, and Japan. Ships from China set sail for Taiwan, where they are given food and fuel on the condition that they do not discharge their passengers on that already overcrowded island. In Japan, friends, relatives, or brokers are alerted to the approximate time and place of a particular ship's arrival. They can then make arrangements to transport the newly arrived passengers secretly and quickly to the anonymity of large cities such as Tokyo and Osaka.

Problems sometimes occur, and police manage to catch passengers who have landed or to stop the boats as soon as they enter the territorial waters of Japan. The media have publicized several cases of fishing boats caught with human cargoes. But for everyone who gets caught, at least some manage to get away. The police sometimes come across beached boats with no one aboard.

Although the number of smuggling cases is small, police sources say they are concerned because, despite months of painstaking follow-up work after each discovered case, they often fail to apprehend all the passengers or the brokers involved.

Unlike foreign workers from South Asia and West Asia—Bangladeshis, Pakistanis, and Iranians—who are almost exclusively "overstayers" or undocumented aliens, the Chinese community includes several different kinds of residents (see Table 2). As a result, the Chinese community will probably see its numbers continue to grow, whatever the ups and downs of the Japanese business cycle may be.

Police sources also note that in contrast to South Asians and West Asians, the Chinese tend to work in groups. For example, they work as part of a team of waiters, waitresses, or dishwashers. Or they may be on cleaning crews that spend most of the night being trucked to public gathering places where cleaning and disinfecting are required by municipal regulations—cinemas, restaurants, pachinko halls. The sanitation companies that hire them are often Chinese-run.

Iranians or Bangladeshis, by contrast, are more likely to be hired as individuals or in groups of twos or threes to work alongside Japanese workers, often for some small parts-maker or in a painting shop with a dozen or fewer employees. They tend to become more integral parts of a Japanese team than do the Chinese, who seem to prefer working with fellow nationals.

CHAPTER 5

Who Hires Foreign Workers, and Why?

Almost all foreign workers in Japan are hired by small and medium-sized enterprises (manufacturers with 300 or fewer employees). Accounting for 70 percent of the labor force, those businesses have been essential to Japan's phenomenal economic growth. But as prosperity grew and the labor market tightened, they became the main victims of younger workers' aversion to 3-D jobs. The story of the Shibuyas (see Box 2) was gleaned over an 18-month period. It is a typical one and demonstrates that many small companies turned to foreign workers because it was the only way they could get the help they needed.

Small and medium businesses hiring foreign workers can be divided between those who hire legal workers and those who hire illegal workers. Legal employees are primarily ethnic Japanese from Latin America (see Chapter 7). The illegal employees are almost entirely from Asia (see Chapter 6). In general, it is the larger companies that tend to hire legal aliens while the smaller companies, such as the Shibuyas' factory, use illegal ones.

It might appear that, other things being equal, employers would prefer legal aliens to illegal aliens, particularly because since 1990 they can be fined 2,000,000 yen ($18,000) for hiring illegal workers. But legal aliens cost more than illegal aliens (see Chapter 7). The deeper pockets of larger companies, therefore, give them an advantage over the smaller companies, which are also in more urgent need of foreign help.

> **Box 2. The Shibuyas' Story**
>
> The Shibuyas own a small plastics factory in northeastern Tokyo, making bottles, boxes, and other containers for cosmetics and office supply companies. They started the company fifteen years ago with Mr. Shibuya running the machines and Mrs. Shibuya taking orders and making deliveries by truck. Although enterprises on their scale are never entirely out of the woods, they have done reasonably well. Gillette is a customer, as is Kao, a major cosmetics maker. The factory is solidly built and well ventilated, but the machinery is secondhand and noisy.
>
> Mr. Shibuya hired his first foreign worker in 1986 or 1987; he doesn't remember the exact year. He hesitated a long time before doing so, but he had such difficulty finding Japanese willing to stay that in desperation he hired a Pakistani, then some Filipinos.Today, although he has dismissed some part-timers because of the recession, he still has seven full-time foreign workers, four Iranians and three Ghanaians. They work alongside Shibuya, his wife, his chief engineer, his chief salesman, his accountant, and a couple of part-time housewives, all of whom are Japanese. The foreign workers came to Japan as tourists and are illegal residents. Shibuya pays up to 300,000 yen ($2,700) per month, a decent wage, but says he cannot afford health benefits and unemployment insurance for his workers. In case of illness, he has agreed to pay half his employees' hospital and treatment costs.

The three major categories of businesses employing foreign workers are manufacturing, construction, and services. A detailed survey of each category, "Small and Medium Businesses and How They Use Foreign Workers," was carried out by Tokyo's Chusho Kigyo Research Center in 1992. Its authors, Takeshi Inagami and Yasuo Kuwabara, found that for most companies, labor shortages became acute in 1989 at the height of the so-called bubble boom, but 27 percent reported they had felt the shortage in 1987 or earlier.[5]

Construction companies said they had been short of help for fifteen years. Typical remarks, sprinkled throughout the survey, follow.

"We haven't had a worker fresh out of school for years." "The youngest worker among our employees is over forty years old." A car-parts maker in Hamamatsu, home of Suzuki Motors, said that of forty employees, one was seventeen years old and the rest were all aged forty to sixty-five years old, including women.[6]

Asked how they had coped with the labor shortage before turning to foreigners, 55.9 percent said they had raised wages; 42.1 percent said they had increased holidays. More than a quarter, 26.2 percent, said they had "rationalized," that is, invested in labor-saving machinery or changed production methods.

Asked what they would do if foreign workers became unavailable, 41.3 percent said they would use Japanese workers. Another 23.8 percent said they would have to reduce their company's size; 20.9 percent said they would rationalize further; and 13.4 percent said they would go out of business (see Figure 2).

The Inagami-Kuwabara survey also shows that construction is one of the major industries suffering from acute labor shortages. Another analyst estimates that 36.6 percent of the nearly 300,000 illegal foreign workers have jobs in that field, compared to 29.2 percent in manufacturing.[7]

The total number of foreign workers in construction exceeds 120,000, including about 10,000 ethnic Japanese and a few thousand students and trainees. There are about 5,500,000 workers in the construction industry as a whole. (Professor Komai estimates that of the 150,000 ethnic Japanese workers from Latin America, 79.9 percent are in manufacturing and only 6.1 percent are in construction—another indication that ethnic Japanese generally have more desirable jobs than illegal aliens.)

In construction as in manufacturing, work is divided up among subcontractors and sub-subcontractors by the main contractors (so-called general contractors). Labor shortages began to show up in the mid-1970s and became particularly acute among sub-subcontractors. These small companies usually consisted of a boss with five to ten workers. The boss would often have to refuse work because he did not have the necessary personnel.

Figure 2. What Small and Medium-sized Businesses in Japan Would Do without Foreign Workers

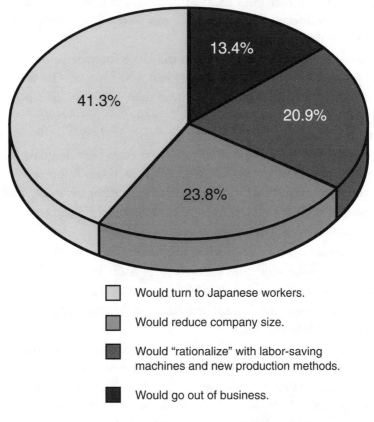

Would turn to Japanese workers.

Would reduce company size.

Would "rationalize" with labor-saving machines and new production methods.

Would go out of business.

(According to Inagami-Kuwabara Survey, 1992)

Compared with other kinds of work, construction jobs are easy to find. Workers are hired by the day and, especially in the years leading up to the bubble boom in the 1980s, have been well paid. Some types of work, such as welding and plastering, require skills that may take months to learn, but other tasks can be learned in two or three days.

However, construction work, particularly at the subcontracting level, has many jobs that are dirty, dangerous, and difficult, and young Japanese have been shunning the field for years. An Iranian told me he used to earn 15,000 yen ($130) per day working for a small company tearing down buildings. That is a very good wage, even for the Japanese, and typical of the booming late 1980s. The Iranian quit after a year, however, when a comrade crashed through two floors and broke a leg. He now works for a supermarket cutting up huge slabs of frozen fish. "It pays less but is safe," he said. But he knows many compatriots who continue to be attracted by the high wages of the more dangerous forms of construction work.

From the employer's viewpoint, as Japanese workers in construction steadily age, a strapping young foreign worker is like "manna from heaven," as one of them told Inagami-Kuwabara.

Inagami-Kuwabara tells of a small construction company in Tokyo that began to hire Chinese students four years ago when the shortage of Japanese workers became acute. The company gave its workers sleeping quarters above the office, supplied three meals a day, and had them work during the morning. They were paid 200,000 yen ($1,800) per month, plus 100,000 yen bonuses twice a year, and sent to language school in the afternoon to safeguard their student status.

By contrast, Komai found that, initially, construction companies paid less to foreign workers, especially to Filipinos, than to the Japanese. But as knowledge of the labor market grew among workers, the employers were forced to increase their foreign workers' wages.

Inagami-Kuwabara notes that because students and other foreign workers are not expected to work more than a couple of years, construction companies often complain that they cannot be trained to do work that requires the greatest skill and the longest training time—steel welding at high levels, plastering, and so on. Inagami-Kuwabara also reports that members of the construction industry widely believe that the labor shortage can only get worse because of structural changes in Japanese industry as a whole. Eventually, many in the industry believe that this shortage will require a decision by the Japanese government to import construction workers on some kind of rotation basis.

Service industries are also major employers of foreign workers. Komai estimates that about a quarter of all illegal foreign workers,

75,000 people, are in the service field as well as the bar, nightclub, and entertainment industry. In the Tokyo area, for example, the food-and-drink business depends heavily on foreign workers. A survey of that area by the Labor Accident Indemnification Council for Medium and Small Enterprises found that 28.7 percent of such businesses hired foreign workers. (The Council is a self-help organization set up by medium and small enterprises nationwide.) In addition to the illegals, many students work in the service field: Komai found building maintenance crews recruiting entirely from Japanese language schools.

In sum, the need for foreign workers, legal and illegal, extends across a wide spectrum of small and medium-sized businesses. The most common reason given by these enterprises for hiring foreign workers is the shortage of Japanese workers. "The overwhelming number of respondents [to the survey] think of foreign workers as auxiliaries to Japanese workers, who in a time of labor shortages are performing tasks that Japanese no longer do," Inagami-Kuwabara concludes.[8]

Inagami-Kuwabara adds that "it would seem there is an unspoken understanding that in a recession these foreign workers can be easily dismissed, and that if so, they can return to their countries of origin." However, although the recession has begun to pinch and there is deep concern about the future, that understanding has not yet led to widespread job loss. As of December 1993, unemployment was 2.8 percent, compared to 2.5 percent a year earlier. Workers who have lost jobs with one company have managed to find a job with another company or in a different field. They are not leaving Japan en masse.

The Inagami-Kuwabara survey also shows that companies hiring foreign workers, whether legal or illegal, are still a minority in all fields, even in construction. If some businesses welcome foreign workers as manna from heaven, others hesitate to employ them. During the current recession, companies are too preoccupied with how to slim down operations, including firing or reassigning Japanese employees, to give much thought to whether they will need to hire foreign workers in the long term. But the debate on the subject continues.

Meanwhile, Japanese managers are sensitive to the accusation that they are using foreign workers as a safety valve, picking up sturdy young Asian workers to replace aging Japanese ones and throwing them away when they are no longer needed. Ryotaro Go, a director of the Tokyo Chamber of Commerce and Industry and president of Nichi-en Chemical Industries, addressed a 1991 symposium of German and Japanese business leaders and scholars on the foreign worker issue:

> When foreign workers come into Japanese enterprises, these enterprises should and must change longheld practices and organizational structures. . . .I think we are going to have to accept that once foreign workers come, some at least will want to stay in Japan permanently. Unless we make the possibility of settling down in Japan our premise, I don't think rotation is going to work. . . .I must tell you that we do not by any means intend to use foreign workers as if they were the choicest morsels at a banquet, (leaving their countries of origin to take care of them when they are old).[9]

6

South and West Asian Workers: Pakistanis, Bangladeshis, and Iranians

The previous chapter looked at the flow of foreign workers into Japan from the employers' viewpoint. This chapter looks at the flow from the viewpoint of the workers themselves—specifically, through the eyes of those classified as illegal aliens. Most came in legally as tourists and, attracted by the huge disparity between personal income in their countries and in Japan, became illegal by going to work. In 1991, at the height of the bubble boom, those illegal aliens came from seventy-five countries, including twenty-one African states. However, the vast majority of illegal workers are of Asian origin.

This chapter focuses on the case histories of a Pakistani, a Bangladeshi, and an Iranian. Workers have come to Japan from many other Asian countries during the past decade: Thailand, the Philippines, or Malaysia, to name a few. Migrants from those latter countries, however, include a large number of ethnic Chinese, who can more easily be "invisible," because their appearance is virtually identical to that of the Japanese. The examples in this chapter illustrate the increasing and increasingly obvious ethnic diversity of Japan's foreign worker population. While anecdotal, the following examples are representative of the majority of hardworking, law-abiding foreign workers in Japan and of the problems they face as illegal aliens.

Until its defeat in World War II, Japan, as an empire with expansive territorial ambitions, treated its subject peoples as second-class Japanese. They spoke Japanese, used Japanese surnames, and bore Japanese passports. But Japan's imperial career began in earnest only at the end of the nineteenth century and was in ruins half a century later. That span of approximately fifty years was too little time for the insular Japanese to habituate themselves to the concept of being a "mother country" that would be absorbing and assimilating large numbers of non-Japanese.

As the postwar treatment of the Korean minority shows, the Japanese returned to the notion that they were a unique, homogeneous people not open to immigration from overseas. Until a 1990 revision of the immigration laws, Japan's basic immigration policy was not to accept so-called unskilled workers from any country. Even that revision gave unrestricted entry only to applicants who could prove they had at least one Japanese grandparent and to the applicants' immediate families.

Nevertheless, a combination of push-pull factors brought an increasing number of South Asians and West Asians to Japan in the 1980s. The push factor, in the case of Pakistanis and Bangladeshis, was population pressure and the saturation of the market for foreign workers in the oil-rich Gulf states. In the case of Iran, the push was the conclusion of the war with Iraq in 1989 and the government's subsequent decision to permit the exit of males who had completed compulsory military service.

Elements of the pull factor were the already noted shortage of 3-D labor power in Japan and the doubling of the yen's value against the dollar. In addition, there was the important loophole in Japanese visa regulations, mentioned earlier. To promote tourism, Japan had signed agreements with a number of countries, including Bangladesh, Pakistan, and Iran, for a mutual waiver of visas. Japan did not sign such an agreement with India, which accounts for the relative lack of Indian workers in Japan.

Case Study 1. *Zulfiqar* (Pakistani)

Both Pakistan and Bangladesh are among the successor states to the former British India. Male workers from the two countries started

arriving in Japan in the mid-1980s as the shortage of 3-D workers
became acute.

Zulfiqar, from Jhelum, Pakistan, remembers the exact date he
landed at Narita airport, the gateway to Tokyo. "September 25, 1987,"
he says. He was twenty-one years old, a junior college graduate from
a modest merchant family. His motive in coming to Japan was to
earn enough money to start a shop of his own in Jhelum, which is
in Punjab.

Several others from his native town had already made the passage
to Japan; some more than once. "If you are expelled from Japan as
an illegal worker," he said, "you are not allowed back in for at least
a year. But in Pakistan, if you give money to the police, it is easy
to get a passport. You go to Japan first under one name, then under
another. Both passports are perfectly legal. Or, you can buy a forged
passport in Bangkok."

Some of Zulfiqar's acquaintances paid a broker for passage and the
guarantee of a job, but Zulfiqar went on his own. He had enough
money for his return passage to Karachi, plus additional money to
show he was a bona fide tourist. He passed easily through customs
and immigration at Narita, receiving a three-month tourist visa, and
promptly disappeared into the countryside. Short, stocky, with a
weight lifter's shoulder muscles, Zulfiqar spent two years in a variety
of 3-D jobs. He was then introduced to his present employer, a company
with ten workers in Oizumi, Gumma Prefecture, about thirty-six miles
due north of Tokyo.

Zulfiqar started out earning 800 yen per hour (then worth $6.40)
washing and cleaning machinery. "After fifteen days, they saw I was
serious," he said in accented but serviceable Japanese. "So they let
me do press work." That is dreaded work because primitive safety
devices make it is easy to lose a finger or even a hand. Old-time
Japanese workers used to say that if you hadn't lost at least a finger,
you weren't worth your salt. Zulfiqar sailed through, however, went
on to welding, and eventually became the night repairman, on duty
every weeknight from five p.m. to three a.m.

With extra pay for night work, he makes 280,000 to 300,000 yen
per month ($2,545 to $2,727). The one-bedroom apartment that

he shares with his live-in Colombian girlfriend costs him 73,000 yen ($663) per month, and food costs another 100,000 yen ($909). His girlfriend was working on an assembly line when they met, but since they decided to live together, she stays at home. "I take care of all her problems—that's the Muslim way," he says.

Zulfiqar gets on well with his boss, and the police do not bother him, "though they know who I am and where I work." Still, he is bitter about his treatment by the Japanese authorities. "I've worked here five years and three months," he says. (The interview took place in November 1992.) Yet he has no visa, no identity papers, and can't buy a car or a telephone or even get a video rental card at his local shop. He is a pillar of his company, the only one still working there out of the ten present when he arrived. He believes he is contributing to the Japanese economy as well. Ten percent of his pay is withheld each month as income tax.

"If I'd spent the same amount of time in Europe or America as I have in Japan, I would have permanent papers by now," he says. His cousin Khowar, who lives in Manchester, England, has a British passport. "But, me, I'm just an 'overstay' to the Japanese."

Case Study 2. *Tariq* (Bangladeshi)

Tariq, from Dacca, Bangladesh, has spent nine years in Japan, and his Japanese is correspondingly better than Zulfiqar's. His father is a retired serviceman who served successively in three air forces—the British, the Pakistani, and the Bangladeshi. Two brothers and one brother-in-law are in the Bangladeshi Air Force today. But Tariq was more interested in engineering than in piloting. With his father's permission he came to Japan in 1984, first to learn Japanese, and then to study automotive engineering at a two-year industrial college.

His student status entitled him to work twenty hours per week. But tuition cost 1,200,000 yen (then worth $5,400 and now worth nearly $11,000) per year, and he ran out of funds before completing his first year. He dropped out and took a full-time job, thus becoming an illegal alien. Like Zulfiqar, he moved around from job to job, observing that "3-D jobs are usually 2-D: they are dirty and difficult or difficult and dangerous. " He recalls working in one factory that was spotless but that required total concentration throughout the eight-hour day. "Otherwise you'll be sure to lose a couple of fingers."

Tariq's last full-time job was with a dyeing plant printing expensive textiles. He stayed two years, taking the first six months just to master the technique. Except for one Bangladeshi co-worker, the other employees were Japanese who had many years of experience. The finished material was used by models in fashion shows and had to be of top quality. Tariq earned 210,000 yen ($1,900) per month for an eight-hour day, six days a week.

For the past year, Tariq has been giving all his time to the Asian People's Friendship Society (APFS), an organization that was formed by a few former Japanese labor union officials and that includes foreign workers and Japanese volunteers. Almost all of its 600 members, who pay dues of 6,000 yen ($54 per year) are illegal "overstayers" from Iran, Pakistan, India, Bangladesh, Sri Lanka, Malaysia, Indonesia, Thailand, the Philippines, and several other countries.

APFS officials want Japan's absolute ban on the entry of unskilled foreign workers to be ameliorated. But given the lack of wide public support, they think that for now the best they can hope for is to obtain special dispensations from the Ministry of Justice for specific cases.[10] In Tariq's case, they hope that his work for APFS will eventually persuade the Justice Minister to grant him such a dispensation. That would regularize his status and enable him to return to Bangladesh for a visit.

At their peak, the number of Pakistanis and Bangladeshis in Japan reached more than 20,000. But since their visa-free privileges were suspended on January 15, 1989, their numbers have declined year after year. Their numbers now stand at fewer than 8,000 for each nationality. (The latest Justice Ministry figures are 7,931 Bangladeshi and 7,414 Pakistani overstayers as of November 1, 1993.)

Case Study 3. *Sohrab* (Iranian)

Sohrab, from Tehran, Iran, had spent twenty-six months in Japan at the time he was interviewed. He has recently left Japan for

Europe, where he hopes to obtain a student visa to enter a British university. He's a tall, soldierly twenty-seven-year-old who was a high school sports teacher in Tehran and a veteran of the Iran-Iraq war. The Iranian government, he said, gives passports only to those who have finished compulsory military service.

Sohrab said that until the Iran-Iraq war, not many Iranians of his background left the country except for political reasons. The country had a good income from oil, and no one felt compelled to go overseas to work. The eight-year war impoverished Iran, and the economy remains weak.

When Sohrab arrived in Japan in April 1991, the visa waiver was still in effect, making Japan one of the few countries that Iranians could enter easily. Sohrab had also heard that pay in Japan was good, so one could make more money there than in America.

Sohrab is one of about 28,000 illegal Iranian workers in Japan, down from a peak of 40,000 before the suspension of the visa-free privilege in April 1992. (The latest Justice Ministry figures report 28,437 Iranian overstayers as of May 1, 1993.) He gave two reasons for coming to Japan: money and the visa waiver. "Everyone wants money," he said, adding, "Japan is a better place to go than other countries. Japan and Iran are good friends; some of our customs are similar."

In general, non-East Asians have a harder time in Japan than East Asians because of their appearance and their difficulties with the language. But Iranians who manage to get over the initial barrier seem to appreciate the greater freedom they have in Japan than in their own country. All the Iranians I have met say that the Japanese police are much less intrusive than the Iranian police, who will arrest young couples for walking arm in arm.

Sohrab told of an Iranian friend who lost a wallet and reported it to the Japanese police. The police found the wallet and returned it to him, asking no questions about his status even though he was an illegal foreign worker. That friend is still in Japan.

Sohrab's first attempt to enter Japan in April 1991 was a failure. Immigration officers at Narita rejected his bona fides. He returned to Tehran and came back after a few days. This time he was successful, but of course his air fare expenses doubled because he made two trips.

He spent four months as a porter at a twenty-story hotel in a Tokyo suburb, receiving 118,000 yen ($1,072) per month, from which 10 percent was deducted as tax, as was the case with Zulfiqar. That is a common complaint of foreign workers: while some are totally unregistered workers, paying no tax and receiving no benefits, most have at least 10 percent deducted from their paycheck. Yet they enjoy none of the benefits, medical or unemployment insurance, that taxpaying Japanese workers receive. Justice Ministry officials, asked about that point, replied that a foreigner should be willing to pay something for the benefit of living in a country with paved roads and law and order.

While working as a porter, Sohrab heard of a job at a futon factory in Misato, a small town in Gumma Prefecture about sixty miles north of Tokyo. He moved to Misato and remained there for the balance of his stay in Japan. The futon business is seasonal and not particularly arduous, but younger Japanese avoid it because of the health hazards associated with stuffing cotton into quilts. The factory at which Sohrab worked had twenty-four employees: ten middle-aged men and women, all Japanese, and four Iranians, including one twenty-year-old woman, the wife of one of the Iranian men. (It is quite rare for Iranian women to be working in Japan.)

The four summer months were the slack season, during which Sohrab and the others were paid only 140,000 yen ($1,270) per month for an eight-hour day. Sohrab spent half that amount on food and on occasional relaxation (bowling). From the fall through the winter, work got progressively busier with twelve-hour days and not even Sundays off at the height of the season. However, all employees got one week off at New Year's, nearly one week off for Golden Week (from the end of April to the beginning of May), and nearly one week off for Obon, the Buddhist festival of the dead (from August 13 to August 15).

Pay during those months ranged from 240,000 yen ($2,180) to 280,000 yen ($2,545) per month, including overtime. In two years, Sohrab said he had managed to save 1.5 million yen ($13,600) while sending an additional 1 million yen ($9,090) to his family in Iran.

The young, husky Iranians work the extra hours when and as needed to keep production in step with demand. Only the Iranians at his futon factory work overtime, Sohrab said. The Japanese work eight hours during summer and winter. Sohrab repeated matter-of-factly what, as the previous chapter noted, some Japanese managers confessed: foreign workers are a safety valve, allowing flexibility in the use of personnel.

"Nobody can live in Japan a long time," says Sohrab. "But for a short time, it's okay. If I had to live in Japan a long time, I would do as the Japanese and work only an eight-hour day."

The presence of the non-East Asians, despite their foreign appearance and the difficulties they have with the Japanese language, shows that in the absence of a rational immigration policy, foreign workers, like water, will flow in wherever labor shortages develop and there are few obstacles. As the influx from South and West Asia swelled, Japan suspended the visa waiver agreements. (The most recent suspension was of the agreement with Iran in April 1992.) Halting the visa waiver has stopped or sharply reduced the flow, but it is no guarantee that some other means of getting around obstacles will not be found.

Iranian workers have told me that since the suspension of the visa waiver, a trickle of Iranians continue to enter or re-enter Japan. Some obtain forged European passports in Bangkok or Hong Kong and enter Japan through airports with relatively few international flights—Hiroshima, for instance.

The non-East Asian presence also highlights the rising visibility of foreign workers within Japanese society. Their presence has roused feelings of anxiety on the part of a people not used to dealing with a large influx of foreigners, though the inflow as yet is not sizable enough to encourage mass protest movements.

A government poll taken in 1990 showed a modest majority of 51.9 percent in favor of accepting unskilled workers on a restricted basis, compared to 24.2 percent against and 23.8 percent who did not know (see Figure 3 below). There are positive signs. People-to-people ties are being formed with the countries concerned, and volunteer groups, particularly among young Japanese, have been established to uphold human rights for foreign workers.

Figure 3. Japanese Attitudes towards Foreign Workers

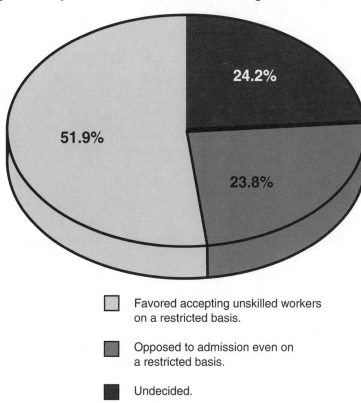

Favored accepting unskilled workers
on a restricted basis.

Opposed to admission even on
a restricted basis.

Undecided.

(Based on a 1990 Government Poll)

CHAPTER 7

Reverse Immigration: Ethnic Japanese from Latin America

"Reverse immigration" is the term used by the author to describe the return to Japan of ethnic Japanese and their families. Almost all come from Latin America, most of them from Brazil. Most of the reverse immigration has taken place since 1990, when changes in Japan's immigration laws made it possible for the children and grandchildren of Japanese passport-holders to come to their ancestral land without any work restrictions.

The revised immigration code was motivated by two factors: the severe shortage of labor in 3-D-type industries, described in previous chapters; and the reluctance of Japan's political and business establishment to open the door to non-Japanese and principally Asian unskilled workers.

Compared to the huge manpower pool of unskilled workers in Asian countries such as Indonesia, Pakistan, or Bangladesh, the number of ethnic Japanese in Latin America and elsewhere is limited. The largest overseas Japanese community is located in Brazil and numbers about 1.2 million, or 0.9 percent of Brazil's 140 million people. Other Latin American countries have a total of approximately 200,000 ethnic Japanese, with 80,000 living in Peru before reverse immigration began. Giving unrestricted access to the homeland, therefore, does not mean that an unlimited flood of ethnic Japanese will rush in.

Since the immigration door was opened in 1990, about 200,000 ethnic Japanese from Latin America have come to Japan, including 160,000 from Brazil and 28,000 from Peru. The number continues to grow, but it is scarcely a torrent.

From the standpoint of coping with labor shortages, reverse immigration is a stopgap attempt to preserve ethnic homogeneity by substituting legal ethnic Japanese for illegal non-Japanese Asians. It may suffice during the current prolonged recession, but it leaves many questions unanswered. Will labor shortages on a scale too large to be coped with by ethnic Japanese alone develop again as soon as the economy starts picking up? Conversely, if Brazil, a potentially dynamic economy, gets its house in order, will it again become a magnet for its citizens now in Japan?

At the same time, opening the immigration door to ethnic Japanese does represent a significant policy change. For the first time, the legal ban on unskilled workers has been breached, in however limited a manner. For the first time, Japanese employers can, and do, recruit unskilled workers overseas, either directly or through employment agencies. The organized way in which some employers have gone about the hiring process shows how acute the demand is for a stable, reliable source of manpower.

No less important is the fact that, for the first time, unskilled workers have arrived with their wives and children, expecting to find reasonable housing, schools, and social services. For the first time, local governments have had to provide language teachers, employment counselors, social workers, and health workers who have some sense of what it means to work with non-Japanese people.

More by accident than by design, therefore, coping with the inflow from Latin America has turned into a kind of contained experiment. It has become an exercise in facing up to the much larger problems that are bound to surface as the number of foreign workers in Japan rises and the lengthening of their stay raises questions about how they will be accepted or integrated into Japanese society.

Earlier chapters have highlighted three problems facing foreign workers in Japan: Japanese ethnocentricity, stratification of the labor force, and integration into Japanese society. These problems also present special challenges for the ethnic Japanese foreign workers.

Japanese Ethnocentricity

Because it tries to substitute ethnic Japanese for illegal Asian workers, the 1990 immigration law itself is a manifestation of Japanese ethnocentricity. But as the Koreans and the Chinese have found, looking like a Japanese does not exempt them from discrimination— nor does even Japanese descent.

Ethnic Japanese of Latin American background say they have had trouble obtaining housing from suspicious landlords. Japanese-Peruvians, who tend to be more racially mixed than Japanese-Brazilians, complain of job discrimination, with some saying that they receive 30 percent less pay than Japanese-Brazilians. Employment brokers say they have been asked to supply Japanese-Brazilians who look as much like the Japanese as possible.

A white Brazilian, the spouse of a second-generation Japanese-Brazilian, says he was asked by his employer to work in a part of the factory where he was least likely to be noticed by visitors from outside.

Stratification of the Labor Force

The importation of Latin Americans has also led to a stratification of the labor force along ethnic lines. In Japan, who you are is largely determined by whom you work for. Whether a white-collar worker or a blue-collar worker, if you are a regular employee of a major company like Toyota or Sony, you are at the top of the ladder. You will get top pay, and you will have job security, which was true at least until the current recession. Less prestigious, perhaps, but equally good in terms of pay, would be a job with a major parts supplier. The further down the chain of contractors and subcontractors you go, the less prestige, the less pay, the less job security you get.

You may actually be working in the same factory as a regular Toyota employee, but if your boss is a subcontractor, your status will be sharply lower than that of the regular employee.

Before World War II, when Japan was itself a labor-exporting country, all workers, from those employed at major manufacturers down to the smallest parts supplier, were Japanese. Regular employees of today's major companies—for instance, those manning final assembly plants—are still almost entirely Japanese citizens.

You begin to notice ethnic Japanese from Brazil and elsewhere as you move down to the next link in the chain—intermediate parts suppliers, some of which may be establishments with several hundred workers. These companies are large enough and financially strong enough to directly recruit workers in Latin America or to hire employment agencies to do this for them. The ethnic Japanese are usually given renewable one-year contracts. Therefore, they do not enjoy the security of lifetime employees, nor do they receive the same unemployment and social security benefits. They are paid close to comparable wages, however, and are eligible for national health insurance.

Finally, toward the end of the production chain come the employers of 3-D personnel—the Asian illegal workers. These workers receive no benefits and have no job security, even though their input is as essential to the product on the final assembly line as that of any other worker in the production chain. They are essential, whether the final product is a car, a television set, or some equally sophisticated piece of equipment.

Zulfiqar, the Pakistani cited in the previous chapter, works in a company with just ten employees, where the boss toils alongside his employees but tells you proudly that he is the subcontractor of a body parts maker for Nissan, Japan's second-largest car maker.

A 1991 survey by the Overseas Japanese Association underscores this stratification. It found 79.9 percent of ethnic Japanese working in factories and 7 percent in offices. Only 5.3 percent worked in construction, where so many illegal Asians work. In factories, 33.5 percent of ethnic Japanese worked for car makers and car parts makers and 19.9 percent worked in electric and electronics companies. Only 10 percent were in the tough and dirty metalworking industries.[11]

Recently, as the recession has begun to hit harder, some Japanese workers who used to man final assembly lines have been seconded to parts makers who used to hire ethnic Japanese from Latin America. These ethnic Japanese have had to find jobs with smaller parts makers or to change jobs altogether and go into construction work or other work they used to look down on. In so doing, they often displace illegal Asians—Pakistanis, Bangladeshis, or Iranians who are at the bottom of the employment ladder. Social workers in the Tokyo area say they are beginning to find unemployed, homeless Asians, although so far it remains true that those willing to take any job will eventually find one.

Integration into Japanese Society

In the case of illegal Asians, no real integration has taken place. The reasons are twofold: their illegal status makes interaction with the surrounding community difficult, and very few have come to Japan with their families. Some illegal Asians have taken Japanese spouses and have successfully negotiated the long, hard path to win legal status for themselves.

In the case of the ethnic Japanese from Latin America, interaction with the majority community is going on despite the hurdle of Japanese ethnocentricity. This interaction is far from leading to integration as yet.

A convenient place to study integration, or the lack of it, is Oizumi, a town on the Kanto plain north of Tokyo. Of its 1992 population of 41,178, just over 6 percent, or 2,468, are registered as foreigners. Whereas the number of foreigners in Japan as a whole comes to barely 1 percent, Oizumi's percentage, which is the highest in Japan, approaches that of some European countries. The largest group in Oizumi numbers 1,382 people from Brazil; the next largest group consists of 289 Peruvians. There are 153 Koreans, 130 Chinese, and a sprinkling of nationals from twenty other countries, among the more exotic of whom are seven Tongans.

Since illegal aliens do not register, the actual foreign population, including underground foreigners, is probably several hundred people higher. (Only one Bangladeshi and nine Pakistanis are legally registered aliens, being spouses of Japanese citizens.) Although it is not unusual to see swarthy-featured Asians at the railway station or bicycling along the streets, town officials refuse to give even estimates of the underground figure.

Oizumi's Japanese population comes from diverse parts of Japan and is more like that of large urban centers such as Tokyo than of its own surrounding rural communities. This is because it was the prewar site of the Nakajima bomber aircraft factory, which attracted skilled and unskilled workers from all over the country. After the war, following a period when U.S. forces occupied the kilometer-square Nakajima compound, the factory was sold to the electrical appliance maker Sanyo, which again attracted workers from throughout Japan. The townspeople therefore are not as homogeneous as most smaller communities, and they are not unused to seeing foreigners in their midst.

Oizumi, along with its larger neighbor Ohta to the north, is also home to a mix of parts makers and small family workshops where foreign workers are most likely to find jobs. Illegal Asians, many of them Pakistanis and Bangladeshis, started filtering in in the mid-1980s. When the immigration law was changed in 1990, many larger factories switched from the illegals to ethnic Japanese. Manufacturers in the Ohta-Oizumi area banded together to form the East Gumma Council to Promote Stable Employment (*Tomo Chiku Koyo Antei Sokushin Kyogikai*) and sent representatives to Brazil to recruit personnel. In one typical case, a paint factory with some 200 employees had been using a large number of illegal Pakistanis. In 1990 it replaced them with 100 Brazilian-Japanese workers. The factory owner was a member of the East Gumma Council.

His factory does the final finish on refrigerators and air conditioners for a major manufacturer. Because of the noise and the fumes, it is a typical 3-D enterprise. When I visited it, the manager said that the Brazilians were doing satisfactory work but that he missed the Pakistanis, who were "hungrier, and therefore worked harder."

In their work with alien residents, Oizumi town authorities make a clear distinction between legal residents, who are entitled to alien registration cards attesting to their status, and illegal or undocumented residents. Legal residents are given all the help the town normally provides its Japanese residents. As for illegals, the town authorities do not want to know about them. "They don't come to town hall, they're not entitled to municipal services, so there's no way we can be in touch with them," said one official.

This attitude has opened up a gap between legal Brazilian residents and illegal Asians, a gap that a citizens' group, the Oizumi International Exchange Society, has tried valiantly to close. It invites legals and illegals alike to its social functions and makes special efforts to keep in touch with the illegals through informal liaison officers— foreign residents who are entitled to be in Japan because they are married to Japanese, they are trainees, or they are in some other recognized category. "Legal or illegal, all foreign residents are members of our community," says Masami Watahiki, Secretary General of the Society, which was originally formed to cultivate ties with foreign countries.

The town authorities' attitude toward the Japanese-Brazilians has been exemplary. Shoichi Mashita, Mayor of Oizumi when the Brazilian influx began, emphasized that the town must offer equality of services to citizens and non-citizens alike. Oizumi was the first town in Japan to provide Portuguese interpreters at Town Hall and to start Japanese language classes for incoming primary school pupils. Its kindergartens and nurseries are also open to foreign children.

There is no breakdown of the effect on the municipal budget, but town authorities note that their extra expenses include the following: one full-time Portuguese speaker and one part-timer to take care of those Japanese-Brazilians who may have language problems; the printing of notices in Portuguese; and Japanese language class in all four of the town's public primary schools.

Despite their Japanese appearance, Japanese-Brazilians are, after all, Latinos. As one official said, the citizens of Oizumi have had to get used to the idea that on summer weekends Japanese-Brazilians may be out on the streets all night, walking and talking and laughing. A samba team in the tradition of Rio's Mardi Gras celebrations appeared for the first time in Oizumi's annual summer Obon parade in 1991 and was a great hit. It has participated every year since then, and Oizumi officials say they hope to make it a major tourist attraction.

Japanese-Brazilians face many of the problems that Asian illegals do, although probably to a lesser degree. According to Mrs. Shoko Takano, who runs the Japan-Brazil Center in Oizumi, a major complaint of her compatriots is that many landlords are unwilling to rent them housing. "They just don't want to rent to foreigners."

Medical expenses are another problem cited by Mrs. Takano. Japanese-Brazilians have access to national health insurance, and in case of work-related accidents, they should receive not only complete medical treatment but also compensation for lost work time. But many employers do not carry the required insurance or are unwilling to give contract employees the full benefits of the law. "They won't do anything until we bring a case to court," Mrs. Takano said. This again causes Japanese-Brazilians to feel they are second-class citizens.

Alessandro Carlo Angeli, a lanky European-Brazilian, and his Japanese-Brazilian wife Lilian Yuriko are examples of Latin Americans who came to Japan with great expectations and are now returning to Brazil bitterly disappointed. I encountered them at Mrs. Takano's Japan-Brazil Center.

Two years ago, Lilian received a visa as an ethnic Japanese, and Alessandro was admitted as her spouse. He had been an agricultural engineer in Matto Grosso, operating a soybean farm that was steadily losing money because of Brazil's hyperinflation and prolonged recession. Although his wife was happy in Brazil, Alessandro wanted to try his luck in Japan; he wanted to earn enough to make needed capital investments in his farm. He took an assembly line job at the Sanyo plant and made nearly $2,000 per month. But this was not enough to support his wife and three small children, the youngest of whom was only eleven months old, having been born in Japan. He quit his Sanyo job and went into the secondhand car business, but the venture failed.

"It's not easy to deal with the Japanese," said Angeli in English. "I wouldn't dream of living in Japan permanently. Everything is too different from the life we were used to in Brazil."

"Discrimination? There was some against me, but not against my wife and children. The Japanese think we're less intelligent than they are, when the only thing wrong with us is that we don't speak good Japanese. They also complain that we are noisy, especially at night. The police came to tell us to shut up, and they were very rude."

Mrs. Takano says "it will take time" for Japanese and Brazilians to get to know each other better. Growing economic recession in Japan has put many Brazilians in Oizumi out of work. "In hard times, we Brazilians lose jobs before the Japanese do." Some, like the Angelis, go back to Brazil disillusioned. In December 1992, Mrs. Takano said, "New Japanese-Brazilians are coming all the time. 3-D jobs are always available, and the newcomers grab them, even though they may be getting only half as much pay as the ones who came in better times." (One worker at the Japan-Brazil Center said he had been offered 5,000 yen, or $45 per day, instead of the 10,000 yen he had been receiving.)

Oizumi has established sister-city relations with Guaratingueta in Brazil's São Paulo State, and many of the town's youngsters are excited by Brazil's vast spaces and unrealized potential. Brazilians, including even the disillusioned Angeli, recognize some value in Japanese-style discipline. But the process of mutual acculturation is slow.

The most telling evidence is that very few Japanese-Brazilians profess any desire to stay permanently in Japan. It is only because of their temporary economic difficulties in Brazil that they decided to try their luck in Japan, most of them will say. In a 1991 poll taken by Oizumi town authorities of one hundred Japanese-Brazilians, eighty-three replied they had no intention of becoming permanent residents of Japan. Seventy-one said they did not think of themselves as Japanese.

CHAPTER 8

Human Rights Issues

The preceding chapters have discussed foreign workers in terms of their nationalities because the different national groups receive different treatment.

All foreign workers also have certain problems in common, though the severity of the problems may differ. They face these problems even when, as in the case of the Japanese from Latin America, there are no legal restrictions on the work they may do. This chapter discusses the common problems under the general broad category of human rights.

Status

The first, and most vexatious, problem concerns the foreign worker's status of residence. Is he or she legal or illegal? Residence status determines the kind of job one obtains and the benefits to which one is entitled, from medical care to unemployment relief. Except for ethnic Japanese and their families, most unskilled foreign workers enter Japan under tourist or student visas that they then violate.

Legally, such overstayers can be rounded up by the police or by immigration officers and deported at any time. According to the letter of the law, it is the duty of any branch of government, including local governments, to report an illegal alien to the Immigration Bureau of the Justice Ministry. But practices differ from ministry to ministry and from city to city.

The Immigration Bureau has 2,000 officers nationwide, of whom 800 are uniformed agents with arrest powers. It has two detention centers with a total capacity of 1,000. It is building a new detention center near Narita airport but lacks the budget to build more or to increase personnel. For most roundups of aliens, the Bureau must depend on the police.

Police attitudes vary from region to region and from time to time. "Overstaying is a crime, and we do not ignore it," a high police official told me. "But at any given moment we have our priorities, and arresting illegal aliens is not necessarily at the top of our list." In general, the police are not interested in overstayers as such, but in whether they commit crimes, such as selling drugs or being involved with the *yakuza*, Japan's crime syndicates.

Interviews with police officers suggest an organization conscious of its need for public support, in contrast to its prewar authoritarian image. The police are reluctant to make a show of force except when the public is clearly on their side, as during the student demonstrations of 1969. All foreigners resident in Japan for more than three months must carry alien registration cards at all times, "but we don't ask someone to show us his card just because he looks obviously like a foreigner," said one high official.

(I am an alien and have been asked to produce my card, but usually for a reason unrelated to my citizenship: because I have committed a traffic offense or am in a restricted area requiring identification. A Chinese illegal says half-humorously that as long as he doesn't ride a bicycle at night without a light, he will never be caught. Even Japanese are immediately challenged by police when they do so.)

In the spring of 1993, police and immigration officers jointly made a number of well-publicized swoops on Iranians congregating outside Yoyogi Park, but these followed numerous public complaints about illegal food vending, traffic in drugs, and telephone cards that had been "fixed" to allow free calls.

Alien registration cards are handled differently from locality to locality. In Oizumi, Zulfiqar complained that without a card, he could not even rent a video cassette. But in Edogawa—a ward (borough) of Tokyo where a foreign worker support organization, the Edogawa Union, is active—and in some other wards, illegal foreigners are issued registration cards with the status column left blank. Police will accept these as valid identification. Nor do these ward officials carry out their legal obligation to notify the Justice Ministry that an illegal foreigner has applied for registration.

A number of voluntary organizations helping foreign workers propose an American-style amnesty for illegals (see Chapter 10). But even without an amnesty, much can be done to ameliorate the treatment of illegal workers in Japan. Giving them valid identification papers would be one way of separating the vast majority of hardworking, law-abiding illegals from the handful of criminals among them.

Medical Care

Illegal aliens are not entitled to enroll in national health insurance. In case of labor-related accidents or illnesses, Japan's Labor Standards Law does not discriminate between legals and illegals. A worker is entitled to medical care even if his employer has not been paying the required insurance. However, illegals are often unaware of these rights. Even when they do know, if they consider the accident or illness minor, they will often continue working because they want the money or fear that their illegal status will come to light. They often wait until the condition has been aggravated to a fatal or near-fatal point.

Ethnic Japanese, being legal residents, do have national health insurance, especially if their families are with them. But they complain that, not being permanent employees, their companies will not reimburse them for days lost from work because of illness or accident (see Chapter 7).

Hospitals used to be able to take advantage of legislation providing for free medical treatment for the indigent to treat foreigners, including illegals. But in 1989 the Welfare Ministry made it known that it would no longer reimburse hospitals in cases involving illegals, claiming that the intent of the law was to help permanent residents only. With the central government refusing reimbursement, the burden has since fallen on the hospitals themselves or on regional governments. There are inconsistencies: separate legislation on the prevention of tuberculosis provides for free medical treatment, regardless of status, for this particular illness.

The law does provide that hospitals should not turn a patient away because he is unable to pay. But in practice, seriously ill or injured patients have been taken from hospital to hospital before finding one willing to admit them. Tokyo and a number of other cities have dusted off a law passed in 1899, which provided for free treatment for a traveler taken ill on the road. Courts have ruled, however, that the law cannot be applied to illegals if they have a fixed abode in the city where they are taken ill.

Gumma prefecture has set aside budget funds to pay up to 70 percent of the unpaid hospital bills of illegal aliens. Some employers have taken out temporary travel insurance for their foreign employees. Some voluntary organizations have created medical cooperatives for illegal aliens. But nothing done so far goes beyond ad hoc measures.

Compensation

Japanese law makes no distinction between legal and illegal workers in cases of compensation for work-related accidents. In practice, foreign workers are often at a disadvantage because they do not know the law. Even when they assert their rights, the employer is often of modest means and does not have sufficient insurance to cover compensation claims. On December 26, 1993, the state television network, NHK, broadcast a program showing an Iranian who had lost both his legs after his truck overturned on a rain-weakened road. His medical costs were covered. But his employer, a small construction company laying water pipes for a suburban municipality, pleaded that any large settlement on lifetime compensation would bankrupt the firm and throw other employees out of work. BRIGHT, a Tokyo-based foreign workers labor union formed in March 1993, negotiated a final settlement of 8 million yen ($72,000) with the employer. Earlier, the union obtained a much larger settlement (35 million yen, or $318,000) from a major construction firm in a case involving the death of a foreign construction worker.

Illegal workers are not entitled to unemployment insurance, and even legal workers may not have it if they enter the country specifying the type of work for which they have been admitted. If they lose their job and cannot find one in the same category, they will become subject to deportation and ineligible for unemployment insurance. The basic labor rights law guarantees the right to organize and to bargain collectively, but in the case of an illegal worker, exercising these rights could subject him or her to deportation.

Nonpayment of promised wages is a frequent complaint of illegal workers, who cannot go to the Labor Standards office to demand payment. Again, the employer is frequently a one- or two-person business and finds it cheaper to declare bankruptcy and start a new firm, or to abscond altogether, than to pay accumulated wages.

The immigration authorities sometimes play a role. Once an illegal is caught or has turned himself in, he is entitled to take his wages home with him. If he has the means, he must pay his own airfare; if not, the Immigration Bureau must pay. Immigration officials say they sometimes call on the employer to pay back wages from which the airfare is deducted and the rest scrupulously given to the about-to-be-deported alien.

Support organizations with Japanese and foreign volunteers have been spearheading campaigns both to help foreign workers and to win public support on all the human rights issues mentioned. Among them are the aforementioned BRIGHT, the Asian People's Friendship Society, the Edogawa Union in Tokyo, and the Carabao Society in Yokohama. The volunteers include lawyers, ministers, labor organizers, students, and housewives; they represent a growing public interest in citizens' movements and participatory democracy.

Marriage, Citizenship, Voting

Changes in resident status arising from marriage or from the birth of children do not affect large numbers of foreign workers as yet but will begin to do so as the number of long-staying overstayers increases. Many Pakistanis and Bangladeshis have been in Japan more than five years and have found Japanese girlfriends and wives. Marriage to a Japanese is legal, even for overstayers, but the application for a marriage certificate will reveal the applicant's illegal status, and he will have to leave Japan for at least one year.

The Justice Minister has the authority to grant special dispensations in hardship cases, and recently the red tape involved has been somewhat simplified. *Nihon Keizai Shimbun* reported on February 10, 1993, that a Pakistani's application for changed status was processed within the record time of nine months, compared to a year or more previously.

As noted in Chapter 3, obtaining citizenship, or permanent residence, is a long, arduous affair requiring a huge stack of documents. Because of *jus sanguinis*, birth in Japan does not entitle a person to citizenship or to permanent residence unless the parents happen to be stateless, as some Soviet-era Russians in Japan have been. If, for instance, a Filipino couple illegally residing in Japan has a child born in Japan, that child will not entitle the couple to remain. But if one of the parents of the child is Japanese, the child has the right to dual citizenship, with choice of citizenship being made at age twenty-one. Dual citizenship on a permanent basis is not permitted.

No non-Japanese has voting rights, including Koreans and other permanent residents, and a long list of occupations remains closed to non-citizens. Some occupations, such as the law, have been opened to non-citizens only after years of foreign pressure and threats of retaliation against Japanese lawyers overseas. Some municipalities now hire non-citizens to teach in public schools. Others still give them only temporary positions.

Koreans and others have formed pressure groups to demand voting rights for permanent residents. Kishiwada, a city near Osaka, has passed a municipal assembly resolution requesting the central government to allow non-citizens to vote in municipal elections. The request has been denied.

Housing

Among the various forms of discrimination, subtle and not so subtle, that foreign workers complain of, the most frequently encountered is in housing. In Oizumi, when landlords were reluctant to rent to ethnic Japanese from Brazil, the mayor carried out a campaign to get the citizenry, including landlords, to accept the Latinos as family relatives come home after a long absence. This was partially successful, but complaints of discrimination continue.

Asians and Africans, particularly those who are darker-skinned, have more difficulty than ethnic Japanese, Chinese, or Koreans. As in India, there is a long history of prejudice in Japan against dark skin. Until farm women, like their city cousins, began to consider a suntan a mark of status, they swathed themselves in long-sleeved garments even when working under a hot sun. Also, Japan has no law on the books specifically prohibiting housing discrimination. Landlords can be cajoled or shamed; they cannot be coerced. This has led some experts to suggest affirmative action legislation modeled on America's.

Women

Some of the most tragic cases of human rights violations involve the most helpless among foreign workers: bar hostesses from Thailand and the Philippines who are in reality prostitutes. Until 1988, the majority of foreigners arrested as illegal workers were women, almost entirely from the two above-mentioned countries.

There is a long history of both male and female Filipinos entering Japan on six-month visas as bona fide entertainers. As prosperity began to diminish the supply of Japanese women in the flesh trade, the Japanese *yakuza* syndicates that have traditionally controlled this traffic turned first to the Philippines, then to other Southeast Asian lands. In 1983, 1,012 of the 1,041 Filipinos and 518 of the 557 Thais arrested as illegal workers were women. By 1988, the figures had jumped to 3,698 out of 5,386 for Filipinos and 1,019 out of 1,388 for Thais. (Among the total number of foreign worker arrests for that year, men outnumbered women—8,929 to 5,385.)

As of the end of 1992, the Justice Ministry estimated that among illegals from Thailand and the Philippines, women still outnumber men: 28,756 of the 53,219 Thais and 18,518 of the 34,296 Filipinos illegally in Japan were women.

Filipinos, coming from a Roman Catholic background and speaking some English, have access to church support groups. The Philippine government also will not allow women younger than twenty-three years old to go abroad as entertainers. But Thai women, who have increasingly replaced Filipinas as hostesses in snack bars specializing in prostitution, are frequently in their teens, come from impoverished hill areas, and speak neither English nor Japanese. Brokers entice them with stories of well-paid jobs as department store clerks or even as models, offer to pay all their travel expenses, and once in Japan, confiscate their passports and sell them from snack bar to snack bar.

The women are virtual prisoners until they have worked off their debts, with the brokers demanding from 3 to 4 million yen ($27,000 to $36,000). In one well-publicized murder trial, three Thai hostesses are accused of having killed the madam of the bar in which they worked. They claimed that all they wanted to do was to regain their passports, which the madam kept in a waist pouch, and run away. It is said that in an average month, more than 300 Thai women seek refuge in their country's embassy in Tokyo.

The silver lining of this sordid story is that Japanese women, who have traditionally been quite passive in terms of volunteer activity, have become active members of support groups such as the Tokyo-based Asian Women's Association. Journalists such as Yayori Matsui of *Asahi Shimbun* have publicized the plight of Asian bar hostesses, and women in politics, such as House of Councillors member Akiko Domoto, have taken up their cause.

Brokers

Many foreign workers coming to Japan rely on brokers of all kinds, from licensed employment and temporary help agencies to *yakuza*-related racketeers and pimps. Strictly speaking, it may not be appropriate to group brokers under the rubric of human rights. While some brokers perform essential services, many tread the shadowy line between legal and illegal to enrich themselves at the expense of the ignorant and helpless worker. Such brokers—particularly those with *yakuza* connections—are often the cause of violations of the foreign workers' rights.

Komai's *Live Together with Immigrant Workers* (see Chapter 5) has a chapter devoted to brokers from Bangladesh, the Philippines, Thailand, and other Asian countries.[12] Twelve to 13 percent of illegal workers arrested and deported in 1991 admitted to having used brokers to enter Japan or to find work there: the actual proportion is probably higher. Brokers in the worker's country of origin will often work with brokers in Japan to obtain necessary papers, including visas, and to ensure that the worker gets on the airplane to Japan.

The worker is met in Tokyo by a Japanese, who arranges work, housing, and so on. Brokers will receive fees both from the worker and from the employer. If the broker is a licensed employment or temporary help agency, the foreign worker's employer will often pay wages to the broker rather than directly to the worker. Technically, the worker is in the employ of the broker, thus sparing the employer the need to hire and fire directly.

The Komai book describes a typical case by recounting the experiences of two Thais, aged twenty-six and thirty-five, whom members of the Komai team met in a town north of Tokyo. Farmers from northern Thailand, they applied to one of the numerous agencies in Bangkok specializing in sending workers to Japan. The agency obtained trainee visas for them and sent them to Japan, where they were met by a Japanese broker and taken to a metal-processing factory north of Tokyo. Although supposedly trainees, they received no instruction either in the Japanese language or about their work as the rules specify.

The employer paid the broker, who in turn paid the workers a wage of 3,500 yen ($32) per day, plus 500 yen per hour for overtime and 800 yen per day for food. These are minimal sums, though they are ten times what the Thais would get in their own country. The workers said they had no idea how much the employer was paying the broker. All the broker told them was that deductions would be made from their salaries until they had worked off 375,000 yen ($3,400) for airfare and other fees.

Ethnic Japanese from Latin America also rely on licensed temporary help agencies. Many employers find it easier to let the temp agency deal with hiring, firing, housing, and other benefits. The employer usually pays standard wages to the agency, from which the agency will deduct its fee before paying the worker. Thus, even with completely aboveboard agencies, it is the worker who ends up the loser.

The recession has made things harder both for workers and for temp agencies. In Oizumi in December 1992, I met one manager of a temp agency who bemoaned the gradual deterioration in the quality of available jobs. Most of his Japanese-Brazilian clients, he said, were used to fairly easy assembly-line jobs. These days, however, the only jobs on offer were in physically demanding and less-remunerative 3-D work.

CHAPTER 9

Policy: The Evolution and Debate

Foreign workers: to admit or not to admit?

The debate on the issue in Japan is taking place in a context different from that either of immigrant-created societies like the United States or of European countries like France or Germany.

Compared to these countries, the Japanese have come late to the debate. As discussed in Chapter 2, during Japan's brief experience as a colonial power in Taiwan and Korea, some Koreans and Chinese did settle in Japan, but there were many more Japanese who emigrated to Hawaii, the U.S. mainland, and South America. Both the Japanese and Westerners saw Japan as an Asian country with little land and much manpower to spare.

When, after World War II, the Japanese turned single-mindedly to economic growth, battalions of teenagers from rural areas poured into Japan's megalopolises. These outsize cities were developing in an almost continuous urban sprawl along Japan's coastline, from Tokyo through Nagoya and Osaka to Fukuoka.

While the Japanese watched as the West Germans imported Yugoslavs and Turks to fuel their own economic miracle, the Japanese had no need to do the same. Japan's population grew from almost 76 million in 1946 to 110.5 million in 1974.

When personnel supplies began to tighten in the mid-1970s as the birth rate slowed and the influx of teenagers from rural areas diminished, there was discussion for the first time of whether and how to procure additional workers. Few, if any, industrialists suggested following the German example of procuring *gasterbeiter*. Instead, Japan became the first industrialized country to use large numbers of robots in the auto, electronics, and other leading industries. It was during this period that the idea of ethnic homogeneity, first promoted during the Meiji period as a matter of government policy, resurfaced in an economic context, with politicians and businessmen taking pride in homogeneity as a major reason for Japan's industrial success.

Given this history, it is ironic that, now that the Japanese economy is mature and the country has managed to come through its period of greatest manpower needs without resorting to *gastarbeiter*, today's Japanese are finding that foreign workers have become essential. Although these workers are still limited in their number, they perform tasks the Japanese are increasingly unwilling to perform for themselves.

In the admit-or-not-to-admit debate now taking place, the two main lines of argument are economic and cultural. The economic argument is straightforward. Proponents of lifting the ban on unskilled foreign workers say that Japan's manpower needs are currently masked by the recession. Once the economy picks up, they believe the acute labor shortages that led to the hiring of foreign workers will resume.

For example, Ryotaro Go, the industrialist quoted in Chapter 5, notes that service establishments, the construction industry, and manufacturers all complain of labor shortages. By the year 2,000, the shortage is expected to increase to 1 million workers. Although Japan's major economic organizations have as yet no consensus on the advisability of bringing in unskilled workers, Go's organization, the Tokyo Chamber of Commerce and Industry, proposes a two-year rotation system for bringing in and training unskilled workers through bilateral agreements with selected Asian countries. Go recognizes that no system will be leakproof, that inevitably some foreign workers will want to stay indefinitely in Japan, and that Japan should be prepared to accept that cost.[13]

Opponents of this economic argument claim that the refusal to bring in *gastarbeiter* in the 1970s was the right decision, forcing manufacturers to automate, rationalize, and innovate—ultimately improving their competitiveness. Today, they say, a new round of technical innovation is required. Manufacturers and processors complaining of labor shortages should innovate or merge or go overseas. If they can do none of these, they should go out of business.

In any case, the supply of workers is not short in the absolute sense: women are still used mostly as part-timers, as are the elderly. More ingenuity is required to make better use of these resources. As for 3-D work, wages can still be a powerful incentive. Perhaps, opponents of admission add, society needs to take a new look at its priorities. There is no shortage of garbage workers, who are well paid; there is an increasing shortage of nurses and nurses' aides, who are not.

The Labor Ministry is a strong proponent of such arguments, as is Rengo, Japan's largest labor union with 8,000,000 members. At the Japanese-German symposium mentioned in Chapter 5, for example, Rengo Representative Toshiyuki Kato sharply challenged Go's proposal that foreign workers should be let in under a two-year rotation system. Japan's work week has been gradually reduced but still stands at forty-four hours, although the forty-hour week has begun in 1994. Rengo's first concern, Kato said, is to maintain the jobs and livelihood of its members. From this viewpoint, "it goes without saying that we oppose the admission of foreign workers in general."[14]

He went on to say, "Labor unions are not progressive organizations. They have a high degree of conservatism—organizations that find their *raison d'être* in seeking how best to preserve the rights they have already acquired."[15]

Opponents of admission buttress their economic arguments by citing the conclusions of a committee commissioned by the Labor Ministry and chaired by Koichiro Yamaguchi of Sophia University, Tokyo, to study the effect of foreign workers on the labor market. A working group of the committee issued a report on July 3, 1992, estimating that the current annual cost of foreign workers to the local and national budgets totaled 6.2 billion yen ($56.3 million). However, it added that if the number of foreign workers who would be allowed to settle down in Japan with their families rose to 500,000, the annual cost would eventually rise to 1.4 trillion yen ($12.7 billion), offset by taxes of only 298.9 billion yen ($2.7 billion). *Nihon Keizai*

Shimbun, which summarized the July 4, 1992, report, characterized it as the Labor Ministry's attempt to show that "if it [admitting foreign workers] is going to cost so much, it's better not to let them in."

The cultural arguments over 'foreign workers go to the heart of the kind of country Japan wants to be. Advocates say that accepting foreign workers is part of the historic process of making Japan a more open country.

Ever since modernization began in the Meiji period, the country has been progressively opening itself up to the outside world. The process is irreversible and Japan cannot go back to being small, self-contained, and isolated even if it wanted to. Given the disparity of wages and living standards between Japan and its Asian neighbors and the enormous population pressures in these countries, some sort of quota system is inevitable. But in a world in which goods and services move freely across national boundaries, at least some provision must be made for freer movement of people as well.

As for foreign workers already in Japan, they are human beings with human rights and must be treated as such. Japan will never be a multiethnic country in the American sense, but it must abandon the myth of ethnic homogeneity. It is already becoming ethnically diverse, at least to some extent—a process that can only add to the richness of Japanese culture.

For example, Junji Ito, president of Kanebo and former chairman of Japan Airlines, says that admitting Asian workers would be one way for Japan to share its wealth with Asians and to avoid becoming the orphan of Asia.[16] Yoshimi Ishikawa, author of the best-seller *Strawberry Road*, based on his experiences traveling and working in America, says that admitting foreign workers will bring conflict to a hitherto closed society, making it more interesting and stimulating. He admits there is racial discrimination in America, but there is also a vigorous fight against it. "Don't worry about letting foreigners in; live with them, and you will find out what that means," he counsels.[17]

"I do not advocate unrestricted admission of unskilled workers," says Hiroshi Komai, professor of international sociology at Tsukuba University. "But the vast majority of foreign workers now in Japan are serious, hard-working people. We should grasp this opportunity to change Japan into a multicultural, multiethnic society that does not reject and persecute others."[18]

Advocates of the don't-let-them-in school, on the other hand, generally cling to the notion that Japan remains essentially an ethnically homogeneous nation. They are in varying states of panic over the thought that the inflow of foreigners is already lapping at the edges of this homogeneity. Many of them oppose not only foreign workers, but foreign rice, individualism, and other so-called manifestations of un-Japaneseness.

The German literature specialist Kanji Nishio is one of the most extreme advocates for this position. Nishio has written books with titles such as *An Invitation to Close the Door on Foreign Labor* and *On a Strategic Closed-Door Policy*. In the latter book, Nishio starts from the premise that when Westerners accuse Japan of exalting its uniqueness, they are equally guilty. Not only do individual countries like Germany or France see themselves as unique, but Western culture itself is by no means universal, because it is the manifestation of Christian culture.

Westerners telling Japanese to become more international or to accept universal values are in fact demanding that Japan accept Western values; Westerners themselves have no notion or intention of opening up the West to the values of other cultures. Why should Japanese stop eating whale meat when Westerners think nothing is wrong with eating beef?

Nishio says there are three reasons why some in Japan advocate admitting foreign workers: humanitarian considerations about Asia's population problems; saving face with regard to advanced Western countries; and industry's demand for cheap labor. But the third reason is the real reason, camouflaged by the other two, Nishio says. For Nishio, what has happened in the former West Germany is a horrible example of what could happen in Japan once the immigration barriers are let down. "[Japanese society] will change into a society requiring an underclass."[19] A helot class will emerge, incapable of being assimilated into the majority society and full of rage over its slave status.

Today, the entry of foreign workers into Japan can still be stopped. But once the notion is accepted that some should be let in, let us not forget, Nishio warns, that "we live next door to a giant country with 1 billion people, a country that can move 10 or 20 million people in the twinkling of an eye." He is referring, of course, to China.

Many of Nishio's arguments are extreme, but bits and pieces of them can be found in the writings and remarks of more moderate opponents of admitting foreign workers. "On this question [of admitting foreign workers] I am a conservative," says former Labor Minister Tetsuo Kondo. "For Japan to rely on foreign workers is putting the cart before the horse," says Liberal-Democrat legislator Jinen Nagase. "We must organize society so we can be self-reliant—though not 100 percent."[20]

"We need more discussion on this subject before we can reach a consensus," says Justice Ministry official Manabu Hatakeyama. Nineteen ministries are concerned in one way or another with the foreign worker problem, and it is the Justice Ministry's task to reconcile and adjust their various perspectives. "We are not a ministry that should lead, that should come out in front of the others and take initiatives. . . . That is a task for the government as a whole. Political leadership is required."[21]

Part way between the pro- and anti-admission forces is a recent book by Tadashi Hanami and Yasuo Kuwabara, sociologists who have written extensively on the foreign worker question. Their latest work, intended to make the geneal public more aware of foreign workers as "your neighbors," suggests that letting in foreign workers does not really solve the problems of small and medium enterprises, because it will keep these businesses from carrying out the improvements that will make them attractive again to Japanese workers. The authors oppose an amnesty for foreign workers presently living in Japan on the grounds that it will drive workers who do not qualify for amnesty into a deeper dungeon of illegality and hard working conditions.

They then propose what amounts to a migration-prevention approach based on a concerted program of investment aimed at job-creation among Japan's Asian neighbors, some of whom, they note, are doing very well while others remain mired in poverty.

The authors do not exclude the possibility of accepting workers from these countries. They do maintain, however, that the program will work only if it is part of a much larger vision that embraces Japan's relations with the developing countries and Japan's contribution to their development. Once this vision is in place, bilateral agreements could be signed with countries such as China, the Philippines, Thailand, Bangladesh, and Pakistan to bring large numbers of trainees into Japan.[22]

The media, which popularized terms such as 3-D, has been neutral in the debate on foreign workers. In dialogues and round-table discussions, often on Sundays, newspapers have given space both to proponents and opponents of admission. Newspaper and television coverage of the plight of foreign workers has been on the whole sympathetic, presenting them as victims of the recession and of an unfeeling government bureaucracy. Mention of crimes committed by foreigners, a notion the police seem to want to promote, seems less frequent now than it was a few years ago, when the inflow of Iranians and other Asian workers was increasing rapidly and public concern grew correspondingly.

However, the media has not used its influence to suggest specific changes in public policy. In politics, 1993 saw the defeat of the Liberal-Democrats after thirty-eight continuous years in power and the installation of a coalition government dedicated to political reform. In the economy, the recession and how to cope with it remain the chief concerns. Unless and until there is another large wave of foreign arrivals, the foreign worker issue is not likely to be taken up as a front-page topic.

CHAPTER 10

Recommendations

Japan is still in the early stages of coping with the inflow of foreign workers. The phenomenon became noticeable less than a decade ago, and the numbers involved are small compared to those of Western Europe or the United States. Government policies are ad hoc, and there is as yet no sign that a national consensus is developing.

As the recession continues, it would appear that the first tide of illegal foreign workers into Japan has peaked. Latest available figures show illegal workers still numbering somewhat less than 300,000. But as joblessness in Japan increases, there appears to be a net outflow of about 6,000 workers per month. The number of Iranians, more than 40,000 at its peak, has declined dramatically.

But in the mid- to long term, the demographic outlook forecasts a continuing decline in Japan's birth rate and the progressive aging of society. The case study of Sohrab in Chapter 6 suggests what could increasingly happen in Japanese society: young Asians working side-by-side with older Japanese men and women. This report therefore concludes with a set of recommendations, or rather of policy choices, for government, employers, and society to consider as they grapple with the task of framing a coherent, consistent immigration policy.

First, attrition alone will not eliminate illegal foreign workers, as the experience with Pakistani and Bangladeshi workers, some of whom have been in Japan for close to a decade, shows. Sooner or later, amnesty is bound to be placed on the agenda.

The pros and cons of amnesty are complex. Not only government officials but many scholars argue that amnesty would only encourage a new flood of fraudulent tourists hoping to be legalized the next time it is offered. Government sources also point out that the vast majority of illegal aliens are single males who in time would bring in wives and children, perhaps parents and siblings. The Yamaguchi estimates cited in the previous chapter claim that the presence of half a million legal alien workers would mean an annual cost to the national and regional budgets of 1.4 trillion yen ($12.7 billion).

However, many overstayers have lived in Japan for at least one or two years, and some as long as seven or eight years. Those who could not adjust to life in Japan have left. The hardcore remain, particularly since the recession intensified. Granting amnesty now would give the Japanese government and society the opportunity to experiment with ethnic diversity in a controlled context. As an island country, Japan's borders are not as porous as those of most other states, and the recession makes it unlikely that a new wave of unskilled workers will develop as quickly as government officials fear.

Amnesty would also solve a problem that government sources acknowledge. As one police official expressed it, "If 90 percent of the people do not obey a law, that law is really not valid." The Japanese pride themselves on being a law-abiding people. For police and citizens alike, the presence of unskilled workers who are illegal but who in all other respects are hard-working, taxpaying members of society creates an acute dilemma. For the workers themselves, the limbo of illegality in which people like Zulfiqar have been placed is very demoralizing. It should not be an acceptable solution, even as a stopgap, to a country that by its wealth and prosperity has become such a magnet to its Asian neighbors.

Second, whether or not amnesty is declared, the government faces increasing demands: even illegal workers have human rights that should be respected. The demands come from volunteer groups, including lawyers who support foreign workers, and, to some extent, from the media. On a whole range of issues—from taxation to nonpayment of wages to accident compensation and medical insurance—laws that make no distinction between citizens and non-citizens, legally present aliens and illegally present ones, are being violated. These Japanese activists say these laws are being ignored by ministerial directives and instructions, some of them oral rather than written. These volunteers call for the government to issue a clear statement that will uphold human rights regardless of an alien's legal status.

The principle that human beings have rights, whether or not they are Japanese nationals, is enshrined in the Japanese Constitution and is being applied more and more widely. But since Japan entered the modern age, there has been a constant battle between the universalist principles underlying Western law and the traditional Confucian belief in the superiority of government by righteous rulers who are above impersonal law. It is only gradually that the notion of universal human rights is beginning to make headway.

Third is the question of how to provide for an orderly inflow of workers in the future—again, a topic on which there is little agreement at this time. The revised immigration laws of 1990 opened the door slightly to more categories of skilled workers, and there are of course skilled workers among Koreans and ethnic Japanese. Justice Ministry figures show that as of December 1992 there were 151,352 skilled foreign workers legally residing in Japan.

But the real argument is not over skilled workers, but over unskilled workers. The Tokyo Chamber of Commerce and Industry, reflecting the views of small businesses that have had trouble finding Japanese willing to accept 3-D jobs, has proposed a two-year rotation system. The Labor and Justice Ministries oppose the proposal, maintaining that greater efforts should first be made to find jobs for Japanese women and older workers. The ministries also argue that a rotation system will not work except in small, tightly controlled countries like Switzerland or Singapore. To these arguments, Ryotaro Go, representative of the Chamber, has said that he accepts the possibility that some workers will want to stay on beyond their rotation period.

Meanwhile, more work needs to be done regarding the definition of "unskilled worker." Studies have shown that while most workers in this category have jobs that require one month or less of training, some do very precise or delicate tasks that need up to six months of training. Tasks considered unskilled in Japan would also be considered skilled in several of the countries from which the workers have come. In any case, it is quite clear that widening immigration doors without including unskilled workers is an open invitation to circumvention.

The trainee program, another source of rotating workers, should be adjusted to take account of the fact that it is easier for trainees to come to Japan from countries with Japanese subsidiaries and joint ventures, such as China and some of the Southeast Asian countries. While medium and larger manufacturers can make use of these trainees, there is a more acute need for them among small workshops with ten or fewer employees. If the training is successful and there are no immediate opportunities in the trainee's home country, he should have the option of remaining in Japan.

Fourth, migration-prevention is an important option for Japan to pursue in concert with other neighbors struggling with an influx of unskilled Asian workers, such as South Korea and Taiwan. The Kuwabara-Hanami migration-prevention proposals mentioned in the previous chapter make an important point: that admission of foreign workers to Japan must be placed in the wider context of relations between Japan and the developing countries. Japan should not be merely importing the most vigorous and enterprising young workers from these countries. It should also be building infrastructure, promoting Japanese-language instruction, and investing in labor-intensive industries, thus creating new opportunities for these workers in their own countries. There should be a progressive transfer not only of technology, but of work opportunities from Japan to the developing countries.

But these recommendations will take time to implement, whereas the need for foreign workers in Japan, though currently dampened by the prolonged recession, is likely to pick up once more as soon as economic recovery gets under way. While every effort should be made to promote employment in labor-exporting countries, therefore, a rotation or quota system for workers from these countries should not await the framing of an ideal development relationship with Japan.

Fifth and finally, Japan needs to develop an overall plan on migration. The two most populous countries in the world—China and India—are both in Asia. Migration from China is already a source of concern, and Japan could well begin to feel similar pressures from India as economic reforms take hold in that enormous country.

Any overall plan should involve cooperation with other rich industrialized democracies, particularly in development assistance aimed at migration-prevention. Japan has a wide-ranging economic aid program directed at Asian countries that focuses in part on increasing employment opportunities within these countries. But Hanami and Kuwabara want a more explicit link between development aid and migration prevention.

A more detailed exchange of information with the Western industrialized democracies would also be helpful. The Western experience with foreign workers and with migration in general predates that of Japan and is broader. Race riots in the United States or in Germany grab media attention around the world, but at both the government and voluntary level, there is much going on in Western countries that Japan can learn from, whether in education or in social and medical benefits or in the whole process of habituating society to ethnic diversity.

For Japan, ethnic diversity is a new and somewhat frightening concept. But in industry, Japanese companies have managed through a process of trial and error to transfer practices that were originally developed for Japanese workers in Japan to developed and developing countries. That effort is being intensified as the high yen drives more and more Japanese manufacturers to open plants in China, Indonesia, and other low-wage countries. The Japanese have had to take account of local cultures, religions, and social practices. There have been failures as well as successes.

Adapting these practices for foreign workers in Japan is a much greater challenge, for it means that Japanese society itself must become more tolerant of diversity. Yet one of the catchwords of Japan today is "internationalization within"—moving from homogeneous single-ethnicism to greater diversity and inclusiveness. Japanese society faces the task of giving substantive content to this slogan.

I am not as pessimistic as some other students of the foreign worker problem. The history of Japan shows that once society accepts the need for change of whatever kind, implementation can be quite rapid.

There are two contradictory aspects to Japanese society: an almost museum-like dedication to preserving old traditions and a frenetic pursuit of all that is new. The concept of ethnic homogeneity has been a powerful energizing factor in Japan's march toward economic superpowerdom. But when it becomes apparent that the concept no longer fits the facts, it is possible that the very people who now see only obstacles to accepting foreign workers may become the most enthusiastic bulldozers of obstacles.

That transition has not happened as yet, but the possibility should not be lightly dismissed. The Japanese are learning the truth of the German saying: "We thought we were importing workers, but people came." And as the Japanese learn, they are having to accept that, in one way or another, foreign workers are becoming a permanent feature, both of their workplace and of their society.

Acknowledgements

I am grateful for interviews with the following individuals, who so generously shared their views and experiences with me:

Ashitomo Choshin; Bae Cheol Eun; Endo Toyotaka; Hatakeyama Manabu; Iguchi Yasushi; Inami Toshio; Iwase Akira; Iwase Takashi; Jaffar; Prof. Komai Hiroshi; Kondo Tetsuo, M.P.; Prof. Kuwabara Yasuo; Majid; Nagase Jinen, M.P.; Ryang Yong Du; Sheikh Ijaz Ahmed; Shibuya Keiko; Shibuya Osami; Sohrab; Tajima Masaki; Takano Mitsuo; Takano Shoko; Prof. Takasaki Soji; Tariq; Udagawa Masahiro; Watahiki Masami; Yamazaki Hiroshi; Yoshinari Katsuo; and Zulfiqar.

I am also grateful for documents supplied by the Ministry of Justice, the Ministry of Labor, and the National Police Agency, and for the assistance of the Foreign Press Center.

At the Carnegie Endowment, Lukas Haynes shepherded my work through from first draft to publication with patience and professional skill and Georgia Levenson graciously took responsibility for distribution and publicity. Without them, this book would never have seen the light of day. Morton Abramowitz, Doris Meissner, and Demetrios G. Papademetriou gave me the idea for this study and encouraged me all the way. What is worthwhile, I owe to them; the faults are all mine.

Notes

1. Interview, Hiroshi Komai, October 25, 1993.
2. Figures from article, Homu Kenkyu, "Treatment and Present Situation of Koreans in Japan," (1955) p. 43. Cited by Hiroshi Tanaka, *Zainichi Gaikokujin* (Foreigners in Japan), Iwanami: 1991, p. 56.
3. Based on an interview with Katsuo Yoshinari, President of the Asian People's Friend Society (APFS), December 22, 1992.
4. Hiroshi Tanaka, "Foreigners in Japan," p. 124.
5. Ibid., p. 74.
6. Takeshi Inagami and Yasuo Kuwabara, 1991. Published as *Gaikokujin Rodosha o Senryokuka suru Chusho Kigyo* (Small and Medium Businesses and How They Use Foreign Workers), Tokyo: Chusho Kigyo Research Center, 1992.
7. Ibid., p. 70.
8. Hiroshi Komai in *Gaikokujin Rodosha Teiju eno Michi* (Live Together with Immigrant Workers), Akashi: 1993.
9. Inagami-Kuwabara, p. 52.
10. Reported in a book edited by Takashi Hosomi, *Gaikokujin Rodosha—Nippon to Doitsu* (Guestworkers in Germany and Japan), Kawai Shuppan: 1992, pp. 114–16.
11. Kaigai Nikkeijin Kyokai, quoted in Komai, p. 102.
12. Komai, pp. 43–54.
13. Hosomi, pp. 90–92.
14. Ibid., p. 139.
15. Ibid., p. 154.
16. Reported in *Asahi Shimbun*, November 20, 1992.
17. Reported in *Asahi Shimbun*, November 22, 1992.
18. Komai, interview.
19. Kaigai Nikkeijin Kyokai, quoted in Komai, p. 102.
20. Interview, September 17, 1992.
21. Interview, September 10, 1993.
22. Tadashi Hanami and Yasuo Kuwabara, *Anata no Rinjin, Gaikokujin Rodosha* (Your Neighbor, the Foreign Worker), Tokyo Keizai Shimposha: 1993, pp. 210–31.

References

Akagi, Kazushige, et al. *Patricio, Brazil Umare no Nihonjin tachi* (Patricio: Brazil-born Japanese). Tokyo: Kashiwa Shobo, 1992.

Hanami, Tadashi, and Yasuo Kuwabara. *Myonichi no Rinjin, Gaikokujin Rodosha* (Tomorrow's Neighbor, the Foreign Worker). Tokyo: Toyo Keizai Shimposha, 1989.

——————. *Anata no Rinjin, Gaikokujin Rodosha* (Your Neighbor, the Foreign Worker). Tokyo: Toyo Keizai Shimposha, 1993.

Hosomi, Takashi, ed. *Gaikokujin Rodosha—Nippon to Doitsu* (Guest-workers in Germany and Japan). Tokyo: Kawai Shuppan, 1992.

Inagami, Takeshi, and Yasuo Kuwabara. *Gaikokujin Rodosha o Senryo-kuka suru Chusho Kigyo* (Small and Medium Businesses and How They Use Foreign Workers). Tokyo: Chusho Kigyo Research Center, 1992.

Karabao, no Kai, ed. *Nakama Janaika, Gaikokujin Rodosha* (Foreign Workers—Aren't They One of Us?). Tokyo: Akashi Shoten, 1990.

Koito, Yuji, ed. *Gaikokujin Rodosha—Seisaku to Kadai* (Foreign Workers—Policy and Tasks). Tokyo: Zeimu Keiri Kyokai, 1990.

Komai, Hiroshi. *Gaikokujin Rodosha Teiju eno Michi* (Live Together with Immigrant Workers). Tokyo: Akashi Shoten, 1993.

Kuwabara, Yasuo. *Kokkyo o Koeru Rodosha* (Workers across National Borders). Tokyo: Iwanami Shoten, 1991.

Meissner, Doris M., et al. *International Migration Challenges in a New Era*. New York, Paris, and Tokyo: The Trilateral Commission, 1993.

Nakaoka, Saneki. *Nanmin, Imin, Dekasegi* (Refugees, Immigrants, Economic Migrants). Tokyo: Toyo Keizai Shimposha, 1991.

Nishio, Kanji. *Senryakuteki "Sakoku" Ron* (For Strategic "Closing-the-Country"). Tokyo: Kodansha, 1988.

Somucho Gyosei Kansatsu Kyoku. *Gaikokujin o Meguru Gyosei no Genjo to Kadai* (Situation and Problems of Administration Surrounding Foreigners). Tokyo: Ministry of Finance Printing Bureau, 1992.

Sugawara, Kosuke. *Nippon no Kakyo* (Overseas Chinese in Japan). Tokyo: Asahi Shimbunsha, 1979. Revised, 1991.

Tanaka, Hiroshi. *Zainichi Gaikokujin* (Foreigners in Japan). Tokyo: Iwanami Shoten, 1991.

Utsunomiya, Naoko. *Nippon wa Yasashikattaka?* (Was Japan Kind?). Tokyo: Kodansha, 1992.

Ventura, Rey. *Underground in Japan.* London: Jonathan Cape, 1992.

List of Tables and Figures